FLYING TINSEL

An Unusual Approach to Teaching Electricity

Grant Mellor

Cuisenaire Company of America, Inc.
White Plains, New York

Acknowledgments

The author extends heartfelt thanks to the many fifth- and sixth-grade students of Huron Elementary School and to the University of California Berkeley Academic Talent and Development Program, who field-tested and helped improve the activities in this book; to teachers Pris Brutlag, Raleigh Ellison, Brad Huff, Alysia and Paul Krapfel, Dan Lewis, Susan McVicker, Jim Miller, Nancy Mellor, Dominic Quinzon, Don Rathjen, Hart Schwarzenbach, Anna Spathis, Lori Thomason, and Tom Wells for reviewing or testing portions of the manuscript; to Bruce Ratcliffe, many of whose good ideas found their way into these pages; to Judy Adams, whose patience and good humor made the editing process enjoyable; and especially to my wife, Sara Mellor, without whose long-term encouragement this book would not have been possible.

Design: Leslie Bauman
Cover illustration: Mona Mark
Illustrations: Vantage Art
Developmental Editor: Judith Adams
Consulting Editor: Ellen Keller

©1993 Cuisenaire Company of America, Inc.

Contents

Introduction

This book was inspired by my first class of sixth-grade students. The school issued them a meager science textbook with a chapter on electricity that consisted mainly of a battery, a light bulb, and a wire. "Connect them together in the right way," the book said, "and the bulb shines. That's electricity. Any questions?"

Yes, my students had a lot of questions. *What do + and - signs on the battery mean? How does the battery work? What makes the light bulb shine? What is 1.5 volts?* The textbook answered neither these nor most of the other fundamental questions that students asked.

I asked myself how I could teach my students key concepts. Then I wondered, "How did people ever figure this out in the first place?" So I began to read history. What I discovered was that history contained some of the very best ready-made science lessons. After all, for a discovery to be made in the infancy of a field of study, it had to be fairly self-evident—or else it would never have been discovered. These lessons had only to be translated into modern language and available materials. I then spent a good deal of time making these historical activities reliable and fun.

This book was born out of an effort to have my students relearn electricity themselves. Students follow in the footsteps of the original experimenters—facing, to the greatest extent possible, the same conceptual challenges. My experience has been that students can handle the challenges, enjoy them, and gain a deep understanding along the way.

Unit One, *Static Electricity*, gives students a firm grounding in the fundamentals of electricity. Students identify two kinds of charges, determine that like charges repel and opposites attract, and discover that neutral objects are essentially a mixture of positive and negative charges. The rest of this unit enables students to apply the concepts they have learned. In Unit Two, *Current Electricity*, students investigate the voltaic pile and current electricity. The purpose of these investigations is to help students to reach an intuitive understanding of voltage, current, resistance, and how they are related by Ohm's law. This is accomplished without using a twentieth-century meter or even a light bulb! In Unit Three, *Electromagnetism*, students continue to follow the historical development of electricity. The first half of this unit deals with applications of the electromagnet, and the second introduces electromagnetic induction.

Whereas many of the lessons are written so that they can be used by themselves, it is my hope that you will follow the book through. But, if nothing else, do have your students fly tinsel, make a capacitor and a voltaic pile, and wind an electromagnet!

Every effort has been made to use easy-to-find and relatively inexpensive materials. As Unit One should prove, good, conceptually-rich science can indeed be done with straws, paper clips, tinsel, and scrap acrylic. Substitute materials are listed whenever possible so that even if you can't find the ideal equipment, students can still try every activity.

Lessons are designed to give students maximum time to investigate in a hands-on fashion. The lessons range from strongly teacher-directed to free-form investigation. There is no one best approach to fit every lesson need. Before you involve your students, I hope you will read the book to get the gist of it, learn the important details, and interpret it through your own teaching style. You are the best judge of what works best for you.

This book may strike the uninitiated as daring—after all, some lessons prescribe shocking your students! Rest assured that each mildly shocking activity can be conducted safely, given appropriate precautions and effective classroom management. As you read through these lessons, you will notice a number of safety rules. Read them carefully and be sure to communicate them to your students before they begin working. (Most important is probably the one-hand safety rule: When students follow this rule, a charge will pass safely through only one hand.) Please try every experiment beforehand yourself, and judge, as a professional teacher, what you and your students are able to handle. And please be willing to accept that there are some students who won't want to try the shocking experiments—be willing to let them observe. In the final analysis, do only what you and your students are comfortable with.

The teacher wears many hats in a hands-on classroom—lecturer, materials quartermaster, discussion facilitator, demonstrator, troubleshooter, and counselor. All of these talents must be put to use in implementing the activities in *Flying Tinsel*. In general, try to let students discover as much as possible, giving as much time as can be productively used in group-based activity. You will have to decide on a daily basis how little to tell your students and how much you can allow them to discover on their own as they work toward the desired conceptual goals.

Three short assessment tests are available in the appendix, each containing individual written assignments and lab practical tests. You may want students to work with partners on these formal assessment tools. But the most valid assessment will come from you—your ongoing, informal observations and formal assignments of your own making. I would like to prescribe one final test, to be used when your students are done with the material in this book. Put a picture of a battery and a light bulb on the overhead projector. I'll bet they will be able to tell you why the light bulb shines!

UNIT ·1·

Static Electricity

What is static electricity, and where does it come from? To answer these questions, let us first consider atoms. All objects, even this page, are made of atoms. Each atom contains positive and negative electric charges—protons and electrons, respectively. It so happens that negative charges repel other negative charges, positive charges repel other positive charges, but positive and negative charges attract each other. These repelling and attracting forces are quite strong. Yet, to the casual observer, this paper exhibits no electrical properties at all. That is because each atom normally contains an equal number of protons and electrons, so their effects cancel each other out.

Let's look at an object such as a plastic rod. Normally, the rod has an equal number of positive and negative charges. Now suppose that we take one or more electrons away from the rod by rubbing it with a wool cloth. The rod would then have more positive than negative charges. If we keep rubbing, enough electrons are removed so that there are significantly more positive than negative charges. Now we can detect an overall imbalance of charge on the rod by holding it near this page, and observing how the paper clings to it. At this point, we would say that the rod has a static charge, or static electricity. An important (and often overlooked) point is that the rod's positive charge existed in the rod all along.

It is common to distinguish between static electricity, in which charges are said not to move, and current electricity, in which charges move continuously around a circuit. The distinction has its roots more in history than in a description of the physical world because, as you will see, static charges move rather frequently. In fact, most of the ideas developed in *Static Electricity* apply to current electricity as well.

In this unit, students learn through experimentation that there are two kinds of charges, that like charges repel, and that opposite charges attract. These are powerful concepts that can be used to explain a wide variety of phenomena. Students also look closely at the nature of neutral objects and discover that neutral consists of an equal mixture of positive and negative charges. Applications of these concepts are found in the latter half of this unit, as well as in many other projects throughout the book.

·1· *Flying Tinsel*

The "Magic" of an Electric Charge

Time **One period**

MATERIALS

For each pair or small group of students:

1 acrylic rod—acrylic is also known as lucite or plexiglass—12" to 18" long and ¾" to 1" around (or 1 large balloon, round or long, or 1 acrylic plate 15" square or larger)*

1 wool cloth (or 1 silk or flannel cloth)*

1 tinsel loop approximately 2" long*

*For teacher also

OVERVIEW

Your students will begin the study of static electricity in an unusual and exciting way when they float a tinsel loop above a charged acrylic rod, as if by magic. This activity demonstrates the curious sequence of attraction and repulsion that takes place between a neutral object and a charged object. This lesson is designed to pique students' interest and to raise questions about static electricity that they will have an opportunity to answer as they do other activities in this unit.

TEACHER BACKGROUND

Vigorously rubbing a neutral acrylic rod with a wool cloth causes electrons' negative charges from the rod to pass to the cloth, creating an imbalance in the rod. Because the rod now has more positive than negative charges, it is no longer neutral; it is electrically charged. The charged rod will draw a piece of neutral tinsel toward it. Once the tinsel gets close enough to the rod, some of the rod's charge will flow to the tinsel; thus the tinsel, like the rod, is no longer neutral but is electrically charged. Because like charges repel, the tinsel with the rod charge will move away from the rod and float in the air. The rod and the tinsel will continue to repel until the tinsel loses its charge, usually by touching something.

PREPARATION

For any static electricity experiments, it is essential that the air be dry. However, since it is difficult to make tinsel loops when the air is dry, you may want to construct a number of loops for your students in advance. You can prepare the loops easily in a humid room by cutting 6-inch tinsel strands and tying them with double knots. Before demonstrating for your class, practice flying tinsel yourself, as described in the following section.

LAUNCHING THE LESSON

Demonstrate flying the tinsel by rubbing the acrylic rod vigorously with the wool cloth.

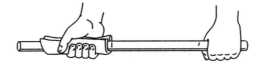

Hold the charged rod in one hand. With the other hand, throw a tinsel loop into the air away from your body. Next, move the rod under the tinsel. The loop will move toward the rod and then away.

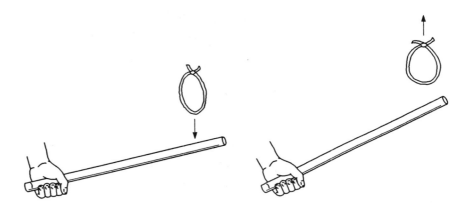

When the tinsel has fallen to the floor, which will probably happen after it touches something, have students describe what they saw and then speculate about what caused the tinsel to behave as it did.

Students can now investigate flying tinsel for themselves. Depending on the number of materials you have, divide the class into pairs or small groups, and give each working team a rod, a loop, and a cloth.

Note: If some students want to try tying their own tinsel loops, explain that dry air can make this difficult, but let them try.

STUDENT ACTIVITY

Give students the following directions for experimenting with the tinsel:

1. Keeping in mind the demonstration, decide on one person to rub the rod and hold it up as someone else throws the tinsel into the air.

2. Take turns with the rod. Share and record any questions and ideas that occur to you as you work.

While students experiment, circulate around the room, giving encouragement and identifying any problems described in the *Troubleshooting* section.

If students are having difficulty in flying the tinsel, look for these problems and offer the appropriate solution:

• *The acrylic rod does not attract or repel the tinsel because the rod is not sufficiently charged.* The rod may be moist because the student has held the cloth too long. The student can switch to a drier cloth and rub again.

• *The tinsel sticks to the acrylic rod.* There may be an insufficient charge on the rod. Suggest rubbing the rod more vigorously.

• *Students wish to make their own tinsel loops and are unable to do so.* Have students cut a 2-inch to 3-inch piece off a tinsel strand and fly it in place of the loop.

• *Neither the tinsel loop nor the short, single strand flies.* The room may have become too humid. Opening a window or turning on an air conditioner might help.

You may want to present students with the following ways of flying tinsel, either as substitutes for the acrylic rod method or as activities students can try right after they fly tinsel with the rod:

• Use a balloon in place of a rod. Although it is somewhat more difficult to use than a rod, the charged balloon may actually make the tinsel float higher. Rub the balloon with a wool cloth, just as you did the rod. Use the balloon to launch the tinsel.

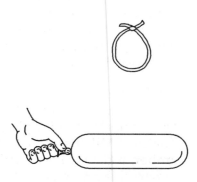

• Use an acrylic plate or a plastic box in place of a rod. This is actually the most dramatic but the most difficult way to fly tinsel. Charge one side of the acrylic plate with the wool cloth, using long, firm strokes. After you have successfully launched a loop of tinsel, you may want to try a straight piece for a more stunning visual effect.

MAKING CONNECTIONS

Have students meet as a class to share their experiences and observations. At an opportune moment, introduce the concepts *attract* and *repel* and encourage students to use these terms in their discussion.

If necessary, help students intuit an understanding of the meaning of the word *charge* by asking questions such as the following:

• *What does it mean when we say that rubbing the rod with the cloth charges the rod?*

• *What does it mean when we say that holding the rod near the tinsel charges the tinsel?*

• *When have you ever become electrically charged?*

Invite students to ask the questions that they recorded earlier and see if they can now answer some of them, either with their original hypotheses or with new ones. Then have someone make a wall chart of all remaining questions and suggest that students see if, by doing subsequent activities, they formulate more ideas about what is happening. As students progress through the activities in this lesson, have them continue to update this chart by eliminating questions they can answer, and adding new questions as they arise.

FOR FURTHER INVESTIGATION

Write directions for these activities on the chalkboard so that students can pursue them on their own.

• Experiment to discover what materials you could use instead of a wool cloth to charge the rod. Decide which works best. (Students are likely to find that silk, saran wrap, human hair, other kinds of cloth, animal fur, and even newspaper or notebook paper work well in place of wool.)

• Make jumping dots. Cut tinsel pieces as small as possible. Rub an acrylic plate very hard with a wool cloth. Turn the charged side of the plate down and hold it over the dots. See what happens. (After doing the jumping dots, students should see that the tinsel pieces jump to the plate and back down over and over again. Students may also want to try this activity with confetti paper, small pieces of foil or paper napkins, paper dots from a hole punch, dots from overhead transparencies, plastic foam packing, or crushed styrofoam cups.)

HISTORY

The study of electricity began with an experiment similar to, but far less dramatic than, flying tinsel. In 600 B.C., the Greek philosopher Thales of Miletus wrote of a substance called electric, which was actually amber, a dried, fossilized tree sap. Electric, reported Thales, had a remarkable property: When rubbed, it attracted, and sometimes repelled, bits of fluff, paper, and similar materials.

This was all that was known about electricity until 1600 A.D. It was then that William Gilbert, an English royal physician, began experimenting with amber.

Instant Tinsel Electroscope

Like Charges Repel

Time **One period**

MATERIALS

For each pair of students:

2 pens, ballpoint or other (or 2 plastic straws)*

l large paper clip (or 1 medium paper clip)*

l tinsel strand (or l strand of magnetic audiocassette tape)*

l roll of Scotch or masking tape (or 1 roll of any kind of tape)*

l wool cloth (or 1 silk or flannel cloth or plastic bag)*

l acrylic rod (or l balloon or any source of a strong static charge such as an overhead transparency made for copy machines, plastic comb, plastic cutlery, or opaque bottom of a 2-liter soda bottle)*

*For teacher also

OVERVIEW

Students will construct a simple electroscope, a device formerly used by scientists to detect the presence of charges. By suspending one tinsel strand from a paper clip, students will make two tinsel leaves hang down. Students will then charge the tinsel, causing the leaves to repel. This activity gives students an opportunity to explore the mystery of why objects repel.

TEACHER BACKGROUND

Because the electroscope's tinsel leaves are really one strand of tinsel, both leaves receive the same charge from the acrylic rod, causing them to fly out from each other. In dramatic fashion, the electroscope illustrates one of the fundamental principles of electricity—*like charges repel*.

The experience students gain from this activity also sets the stage for Lesson 4, in which they charge each of two separate tinsels with a different charge agent and see that they attract. In light of the present lesson, students will be able to recognize the attraction as a curious and significant event. Lessons 4, 5, and 8 will shed some light on why charged objects attract and repel.

PREPARATION

Construct an electroscope, following the directions given in the *Student Activity* section of this lesson, and test it out before working with the students. The tinsel leaves should first fly away from the rod and then fly apart from each other. Ground, or neutralize, the electroscope by touching the paper clip with a finger. The charge trapped in the electroscope will now escape through your finger, causing the tinsel to become neutral and to hang straight down.

LAUNCHING THE LESSON

Ask students to recall what happened when they experimented with two different objects, the tinsel and the rod, in the previous lesson. Then tell students that they are going to carry out another activity that may give them some ideas about why certain objects repel each other.

Mention that scientists formerly used a device called an electroscope when they wanted to detect the presence of electricity. Suggest that students work in pairs to make their own electroscope while you demonstrate each step by constructing one of your own.

STUDENT ACTIVITY

Give students the following directions for constructing the electroscope:

1. Tape two pens together to form one long pen.

2. Partly unfold the paper clip. Slip the larger end around the pocket tab of the pen cap.

3. Use a single knot to tie the tinsel to the paper clip. Be careful not to stretch the tinsel.

4. Straighten the tinsel leaves so that they hang next to each other without tangling. The electroscope is now complete and ready to use.

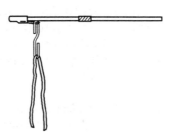

Have one student hold the electroscope while the other follows these directions:

5. Begin by charging the acrylic rod with your cloth.

6. Predict what will happen when you hold the acrylic rod near the tinsel leaves.

7. Hold the charged rod near the tinsel. How do your predictions match what happened?

8. Touch the paper clip with your finger.

9. Now change positions with your partner. Whoever held the electroscope should now charge the rod.

10. Touch the rod to the top of the paper clip. What happens?

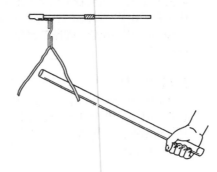

Troubleshooting

If an electroscope doesn't work, look for the following problems:

• *The tinsel may be stretched at the knot.* The tinsel's conductive coating may be broken. Replace the tinsel.

• *The knot may be too loose.* Replace the tinsel and tie a simple knot, pulling the tinsel snugly against the clip while taking care not to stretch it.

• *The tinsel may be tangled.* Straighten the tinsel leaves.

• *The pens or substitute materials may not be good insulators.* If you suspect this is the case, have students with this problem start over with different pens and new tinsel.

MAKING CONNECTIONS

Talk with the whole class, using questions such as the following to focus students' thinking:

• *What happened when you experimented with the electroscope?*

• *What do you think made the two halves of the tinsel fly apart from each other?*

• *Why do you think the tinsel loop in Lesson 1 might have been repelled by the acrylic rod?*

• *Based on the two experiments you have done so far, what new ideas occur to you?*

Help students to realize that in both cases a single piece of tinsel received a charge from an acrylic rod and that similarly charged objects repelled each other.

Point out that an object stays charged until the charge can leave it. Ask someone to recall what happened with the electroscope. (When students touched the paper clip with one finger, they grounded the electroscope, or allowed the electrical charge to leave it.)

FOR FURTHER INVESTIGATION

Write directions for these activities on the chalkboard so that students can pursue them on their own.

• Discover how long the leaves of the electroscope will stay apart. Observe and record the length of time. See whether it remains the same when you charge the electroscope on two or three different occasions. Think about why or why not.

• Set up an electroscope under different weather conditions and observe the results. What happens when the weather is humid? Dry and cold? Dry and warm? What effect will a steamy bathroom have on the electroscope?

HISTORY

Electroscopes were used extensively by the early scientists who investigated electricity, including Benjamin Franklin and Alessandro Volta. Extraordinarily sensitive electroscopes that use gold foil leaves are made even today.

·3· Here a Charge, There a Charge

Everywhere a Charge!

Time **One period**

MATERIALS

For each small group of students:

2 plastic straws (or 2 plastic pens taped together, plastic spatula, acrylic rod, or plastic ruler)*

1 tinsel strand (or small ball of aluminum foil suspended by a string)*

l wool cloth (or flannel, silk or nylon cloth or plastic bag)*

l small piece of masking tape*

1 book for holding charge tester in place

scissors

For the whole class:
A mixture of classroom objects, some of which will produce a charge, some of which will not: For example, a book jacket, pen, pencil, plastic coat hanger, metal coat hanger, plastic cutlery and cups, wooden ruler, shoe, trash can, balloon.

*For teacher also

OVERVIEW

Students will make tinsel charge testers to use with a variety of objects around the classroom. In using them, students will discover that many neutral objects are capable of producing a moderate or strong charge when rubbed with wool, whereas others produce a weak charge or none at all.

TEACHER BACKGROUND

We can turn a piece of tinsel into a fairly sensitive static charge-detector by suspending it from a plastic straw. The straw acts as an insulator, or nonconductor, which prevents electricity from passing through. The tinsel can remain charged even when attached to the straw.

When any charged object, for example, a coat hanger, is brought near, the tinsel reacts as it did to the acrylic rod. First, the tinsel is attracted to the hanger. Then, if the hanger is sufficiently charged, the tinsel is repelled. This happens when there is enough charge on the object for some to be transferred to the tinsel; both objects then have the same charge.

In this activity, students will make three different observations: An uncharged object will not affect the tinsel at all; a charged object will attract the tinsel; a strongly charged object will first attract and then repel the tinsel.

PREPARATION

Make a charge tester by setting up two straws and the tinsel as shown in the *Student Activity* section, steps 1-4. Place three objects nearby: 1. a plastic coat hanger, which will produce a strong charge, causing the tinsel to attract and repel, 2. a plastic comb, which will produce a weak charge, causing the tinsel only to attract, and 3. a wooden or metal ruler, which will cause no reaction at all.

LAUNCHING THE LESSON

Arouse students' interest by bringing the charged plastic coat hanger underneath the tinsel hanging from the straw. Students will see that the coat hanger first attracts and then repels the tinsel. You can make the tinsel stand straight up and "dance" by moving the hanger back and forth below it. Mention that we can call the straw and tinsel a charge tester.

Point out the other two objects nearby. Ask students to predict what will happen when you rub them with a wool cloth and then wave them under the tinsel. Be sure students give reasons for their opinions. Ground the tinsel by touching it and then demonstrate with the two remaining objects.

Have students describe the three kinds of results they observed. Then enlist students' suggestions for setting up a three-column chart on the chalkboard to show the various categories of objects tested. The chart could be similar to the one in the illustration below.

Strongly-charged	Weakly-charged	No charge

Tell students they are now going to make their own charge testers with straws and tinsel. Organize students in small groups so that they can share objects and discuss what they observe as they work with their own charge testers.

STUDENT ACTIVITY

First, have students prepare their charge testers by following these steps:

1. Put two straws together by sticking the end of one into the other, to make one long straw.

2. Place one end of the long straw under a book on the edge of a table, desk, or chair.

3. Use a piece of tape half the size of a dime to attach the tinsel to the straw.

4. Snip the tinsel so that it is too short for the loose end to touch the table when it flies out.

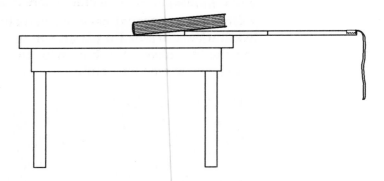

If they like, students can prepare their own data record sheets, using the chart you created together on the chalkboard.

Before actual testing begins, have pairs of students choose the first object for testing, rub the object very hard with a wool cloth and then bring the object slowly to the tinsel, observing the reaction.

As they work, remind students that if the object attracts the tinsel, it has produced a weak charge; if it attracts and then repels the tinsel, it has produced a greater charge; if the tinsel does not move, the object has not produced any charge at all.

When everyone has finished testing one object, have the class share its observations. Then give students these directions to follow:

5. Work individually or in pairs within a group to test and record results with as many classroom objects as you can in 15-20 minutes. Record your results.

6. Compile a group chart from your individual data record sheets. Identify any results that differ with a question mark. *Remember to ground the tinsel by touching it before every test.*

Troubleshooting

While students are testing objects, circulate and observe testing techniques. Be on the lookout for two potential problems producing false results:

• *An object appears to be strongly charged when in reality it isn't.* A very slight draft in the classroom can move the tinsel and give a false reading. Locate and eliminate the draft.

• *An object appears to contain some charge when it doesn't.* The tinsel was not grounded by touching after the previous object was tested. A non-grounded tinsel will even be attracted to fingers. Remind students to ground the tinsel.

MAKING CONNECTIONS

One student from each group should record the compiled data, including question marks, on the class chart that you began on the chalkboard. In discussing class results, do some of the following:

• Use the chart to discuss the similarities and discrepancies in the class results. Individuals can retest objects for which the results are in doubt, and the class can then decide where those items belong on the chart.

• Once consensus has been reached about each item on the master chart, ask students to look for patterns in the data. Are there similarities among the charged objects? What about the uncharged objects? Students may notice that some of the strongly charged objects are made of plastic. They may be surprised to find that none of the metals produced a charge.

• Ask students to explain what *grounding* means and how they grounded objects. Help students to understand that touching a charged object allows the charge to leave that object.

Guide students as they pull together all the ideas they have learned in the first three activities. These might include the following:

• An object (such as the rod) can be charged by rubbing.

• An object (such as tinsel) can be charged by touching the charged rod. (Students may or may not realize that some of the charge can be transferred.)

• A charged object attracts a neutral object.

• A variety of objects produce a charge.

• Two charged objects repel (this idea will be modified later).

• An object can be neutralized by being touched.

FOR FURTHER INVESTIGATION
Write directions for these activities on the chalkboard so that students can pursue them on their own:

• Make two charge testers. Use straws and tinsel to make them. Place the charge testers far apart. Charge both with a charged acrylic rod. Then bring the charge testers together. What happens?

• Find charges around the house. Make a charge tester at home. Look for objects in your house that you think can be strongly—or weakly—charged. Test them. Did anything surprise you by the way it reacted? Can you figure out why those objects behaved as they did?

·4· *An Unexpected Reaction*

Attracting and Repelling

Time **One period**

MATERIALS

For each small group of students:

4 plastic straws (or any long plastic objects such as a spatula or a pen)*

2 tinsel strands*

1 acrylic rod (or glass rod or overhead transparency)*

1 inflated balloon (or 1 Bic™ pen, opaque base from 2-liter soda bottle, plastic cutlery, or plastic gallon milk jug)*

1 roll of masking tape*

2 books for holding charge testers in place

2 wool cloths (or 2 silk cloths or plastic bags)*

various charge-producing objects identified on the list from Lesson 3

*For teacher also

OVERVIEW

As you move two charged tinsels slowly together, students will probably predict, based on their previous experience in the first three lessons, that the tinsels will repel. What then occurs may strike students as a mistake on your part: The tinsels attract! When students repeat your demonstration by charging one tinsel with an acrylic rod and another with a balloon, much to their surprise, students' tinsels strongly attract also.

This experience prompts a closer look at the charges on the rod and the balloon. Students quickly build a catalog of facts: A charged rod repels the rod-charged tinsel; a charged balloon repels the balloon-charged tinsel; a charged rod attracts the balloon-charged tinsel; and a charged balloon attracts the rod-charged tinsel.

In light of this new development, students are prompted to see how other charged objects behave. Using the balloon-charged tinsel and the rod-charged tinsel as investigative tools, students determine that all charged objects behave either like the charged rod or the charged balloon.

At the end of the lesson you will help students to express their experimental results in modern terms. You will call the two charged groups not *rod* and *balloon* but *positive* and *negative*. The relationship between charges is usually stated succinctly in this manner: *like charges repel; opposites attract.*

TEACHER BACKGROUND

From a conceptual standpoint, this may be the most important lesson in this book. Whereas most students are simply told that there are positive and negative charges, here students will test out this assertion themselves. In fact, they will be retracing the steps of the original discoverers, who also discerned two groups of charges and named these groups positive and negative. See the *Making Connections* and *History* sections of this lesson for more information.

PREPARATION

Construct two tinsel charge-testers as described in the *Student Activity* section, steps 1-3. Have an acrylic rod and an inflated balloon nearby as you begin.

LAUNCHING THE LESSON

Following the procedure outlined in the *Student Activity* section, steps 4 and 5, charge your two charge testers, one with the acrylic rod, the other with the balloon. Ask students what they would expect to happen if you were to bring the two charged tinsels together. Based on earlier experiences with the electroscope and the tinsel charge-tester, students will probably expect the tinsels to repel. Now bring the tinsels together and demonstrate that the charged tinsels are attracted to each other.

You may want to "ham it up" and act surprised, as if the two tinsels should not have attracted. Next, ask students to experiment themselves to see whether your result was caused by an error in your procedure.

STUDENT ACTIVITY

Have students working in small groups, and follow steps 1-6 as they make and then test charge testers:

1. For each charge tester, insert the end of one straw into another. With a very small piece of tape, attach a tinsel to one end of each extended straw.

2. Place the two charge testers about a meter, or 39 inches, apart and use books to hold them in place.

3. Cut the tinsel so that the loose ends don't touch the table when they fly out.

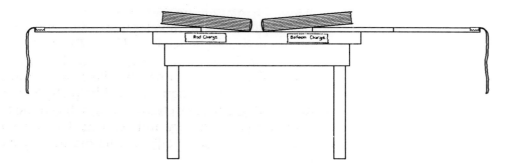

4. Charge one tinsel with an acrylic rod and then label it by writing "Rod Charge" on a strip of tape stuck to the table near the straw. Test to see if the tinsel is properly charged by holding the acrylic rod at an angle near the tinsel. The rod should repel the tinsel.

5. Now charge the other tinsel with a balloon and label it "Balloon Charge." Test this tinsel for charge with the balloon. (If the tinsel is properly charged, the balloon should repel the tinsel also.)

6. Predict what will happen when you move the straws slowly together. Then do so and describe what happens. (The straws attract.)

7. Ground, then recharge, the tinsels with their respective charges (balloon and rod). Bring the charged rod to each tinsel one at a time. Observe what happens and record your results. (Students should be able to see that the charged rod repels the rod-charged tinsel and attracts the balloon-charged tinsel.)

8. Ground and recharge the two tinsels again. Now bring the charged balloon to each tinsel one at a time. Observe what happens and record your results. (Students should be able to see that the charged balloon repels the balloon-charged tinsel and attracts the rod-charged tinsel.)

Now, guide students through the following procedure for using their charge testers to test more objects:

9. Look at the list of charge-producing objects you made for Lesson 3. Find those objects identified as strong charge-producers. You are going to test these objects with a balloon-charged and a rod-charged tinsel.

10. Predict how these objects will actually behave when held near a balloon-charged object and a rod-charged object. Will these objects attract both the balloon-charged tinsel and the rod-charged tinsel? Will they repel them both? Will they attract one and repel the other? Prepare to find out!

11. As the first step, quickly draw up a data sheet to record your findings. Display the following graphic for students to copy:

Rod Charge	Balloon Charge
1.	1.
2.	2.
3.	3.
4.	4.
5.	5.

12. Before you begin your investigation, ground and then recharge your balloon and rod tinsels with your two charge sources.

13. Choose one of the objects that became strongly charged in Lesson 3. Charge it with a wool cloth and bring it slowly to the balloon-charged tinsel. Observe how the object behaves and then record the name of the object under one of the headings on the data sheet.

14. Recharge the object and bring it slowly to the rod-charged tinsel. Again, record the result.

15. Follow the same procedure for several other objects you used in Lesson 3. *Be sure to ground the tinsels and recharge them (one with the acrylic rod and the other with the balloon) each time before charging them with another object.*

While students are experimenting, circulate among them to offer assistance.

Troubleshooting

If the students work carefully, they should find that every item they test belongs either to the rod- or the balloon-charged group. Here are some erroneous assumptions students might make:

• *Students conclude that an object belongs to neither charge group because it attracts both the rod-charged and the balloon-charged tinsels.* It is likely that students have not adequately charged the object they are testing. Remind them that the tinsels are themselves charged, and that a charged tinsel is attracted to any uncharged object (as they learned by flying tinsel in the first lesson). Suggest that students rub the object more vigorously and try again.

• *Students conclude that the object belongs to neither group, or both groups, because it repels both the balloon-charged and the rod-charged tinsels.* Students have neglected to ground and recharge the tinsels at the beginning of every test. Encourage the group to carefully ground tinsels, rub the acrylic rod and balloon again, and recharge the two tinsels before repeating the test.

MAKING CONNECTIONS

On the chalkboard, make a list of students' initial observations:

• Charged rod repels rod-charged tinsel.

• Charged rod attracts balloon-charged tinsel.

• Charged balloon attracts rod-charged tinsel.

Tell students that all of this is usually expressed as *like charges repel; opposites attract.*

Also on the chalkboard, make a chart with three categories: *Rod Charge, Balloon Charge,* and *Other.* Have students from each group record their data on the chart. Then ask them to retest any items in the *Other* category, as well as any other items for which results vary. Eventually, the class should reach a consensus that every object capable of producing a charge when rubbed belongs to either the rod group or the balloon group.

Ask students how many different kinds of charges there appear to be and why do they think so. Students should come to see that each charged object seems to have the same kind of charge as either the rod charge or the balloon charge.

Tell students that almost two and a half centuries ago scientists performed a similar experiment and came up with the same conclusions. Instead of calling their groups *rod charge* and *balloon charge*, the scientists called them *vitreous* and *resinous*. Benjamin Franklin decided to rename the two groups *positive* and *negative*, respectively. Explain that Franklin assigned these terms more or less randomly, but they have become standard. Ask students to write *Positive* above *Rod* on their charts, and *Negative* above *Balloon*.

Because this is a fairly complex lesson, it is worth summarizing the results. On the chalkboard, restate students' observations in modern terminology:

- There are two kinds of charges—positive and negative.
- Positive repels positive.
- Negative repels negative.
- Negative attracts positive.
- Positive attracts negative.
- Like charges repel; opposites attract.

HISTORY

In the middle of the eighteenth century, scientists discovered that every charged object they knew of could be placed into one of two groups which they called *vitreous* (meaning glasslike) and *resinous* (resin-like). They determined that a charged object in the vitreous group repelled any other charged object in the vitreous group. Similarly, any charged object in the resinous group repelled any other object in the resinous group. (Like charges repel.) The scientists also discovered that any charged object in the vitreous group attracted any charged object in the resinous group. (Opposites attract.) Benjamin Franklin experimented and renamed the two kinds of charges *positive* and *negative*.

5

The Nature of Neutral

A Mixture of Charges

Time **One or two periods**

MATERIALS
For each small group of students:

4 plastic straws*

2 tinsel strands*

2 acrylic rods (or 1 glass rod or any object from Lesson 4 that produces a positive rod-charge)*

1 inflated balloon (or 1 Bic™ pen, plastic cutlery or any object from Lesson 4 which produces a negative balloon-charge)*

1 roll of masking tape*

2 books for holding charge testers in place

2 wool cloths*

1 empty plastic 2-liter soda bottle with top screwed on

various charge-producing objects identified on the list from Lesson 4

*For teacher also

OVERVIEW
Students will begin this lesson by once again bringing two oppositely-charged tinsels into contact with each other to make neutral tinsel. Students will then reverse this process by rubbing together two neutral objects—an acrylic rod and a plastic bottle—and charging them both. Students will discover that when an acrylic rod is rubbed with a plastic bottle, the rod becomes positively charged and the bottle becomes negatively charged. The advantage of using a bottle rather than a cloth is that students can much more easily detect the charge on the plastic.

TEACHER BACKGROUND
At this moment, you probably have a *neutral,* or uncharged pencil, nearby. Does *neutral* mean that the pencil has no positive or negative charges or that it contains an equal number of positive and negative charges? This question is probably easy for you to answer: All objects are made of atoms, which are an equal mix of positive and negative charges (residing in protons and electrons, respectively). So, it follows that neutral objects are a combination of positive and negative. To students, however, the answer is not so obvious. Some may believe that neutral is a mix of positive and negative charges (especially after the last lesson, in

which students saw a positive and a negative charge become neutral). But other students may have a "common sense" view that a neutral object has an absence of charge. The purpose of this lesson is to get students to believe that neutral is an even mix of positive and negative.

PREPARATION

Write the following questions on the chalkboard for students to consider:

What does it mean to say that something is neutral, or uncharged?
Does a neutral object have a charge?
Where do electric charges come from?

Construct two charge testers like those you made in Lesson 4. This time, try to cut the tinsels to nearly the same length.

LAUNCHING THE LESSON

Review part of Lesson 4 by charging one tinsel charge-tester with an acrylic rod and the other with a balloon. Slowly bring the two tinsels together. Students should see that the tinsels attract and then fall neutral (or nearly so). Have students test the tinsels with a finger to show that they are neutral.

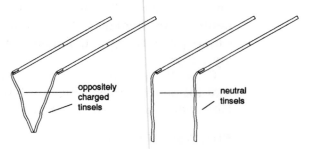

oppositely charged tinsels

neutral tinsels

Have students read the questions that you wrote on the chalkboard. Solicit ideas about possible answers and write them on the chalkboard. Explain to students that they will now conduct an experiment designed to help them answer these questions.

STUDENT ACTIVITY

Begin by providing these instructions for students to follow:

1. Construct and label two charge testers as you did in Lesson 4.

2. Remove the charge on the acrylic rod by rubbing your hand over the rod.

3. Recharge your rod, but this time substitute the plastic bottle for the wool cloth. Rub the rod vigorously along the side of the bottle.

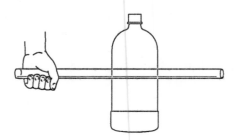

4. Use the charge testers to determine what charge the rod now has and what charge the bottle now has. (The rod should be positively charged and the bottle negatively charged.)

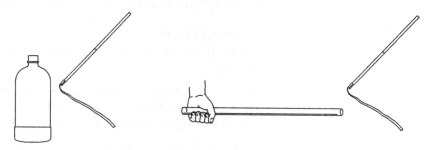

MAKING CONNECTIONS

Recount with the class what they have seen: First, two oppositely-charged tinsels touched and became neutral. Next, two neutral objects—the rod and the bottle—were rubbed together and became oppositely charged.

Discuss the questions posed at the beginning of the session. As suggested earlier, some students may feel strongly that a neutral object has no charge at all. Others may suspect, in light of their experiments, that neutral must contain both positive and negative charges. Both positions can be strongly argued. Encourage students to "take sides" for an enriching debate.

Close the lesson by explaining that the consensus among scientists is that all neutral objects are a mixture of positive and negative charges. However, since these charges are balanced, we are unable to detect them.

FURTHER INVESTIGATION

Encourage students to read and report back about atoms and their component parts: protons, neutrons, and electrons. (Students should find that every neutral atom has an equal number of protons and electrons, or positive and negative charges.)

6

Imbalancing Act

Separating Charges within a Neutral Object

Time **One or two periods**

MATERIALS

For each small group of students:

4 plastic straws (or any plastic object such as a pen, spatula, or ruler)*

2 tinsel strands*

1 acrylic rod (or any positive charge source such as a glass rod or some brands of overhead transparencies)

1 balloon (or any negative charge source such as a Bic™ pen, plastic comb, or plastic cutlery)

2 small pieces of masking tape*

1 wool cloth*

For *Launching the Lesson*:

1 soda can

1 balloon

1 tinsel loop

1 acrylic rod

1 wool cloth

*For teacher also

OVERVIEW

Students participate in a demonstration in which neutral objects attract charged objects. They then use a charged acrylic rod to separate positive and negative charges within a piece of tinsel. (This process—*electrostatic induction*—is explained below.) Students also use a positively-charged source to charge an object negatively.

TEACHER BACKGROUND

Let us reconsider the first lesson, in which students flew loops of tinsel above a charged acrylic rod. We can explain why the tinsel floats above the rod: We say "like charges repel." But we still haven't explained why the tinsel is first attracted to the rod. Nor have we explained why the tinsel, once charged, will stick to the ceiling or wall. We need to answer the important question "Why are neutral objects attracted to charged objects?"

The answer lies in a phenomenon called *electrostatic induction*, in which charges within a neutral object become separated, or imbalanced, when placed near an external source of charge. The object still has an equal number of positive and negative charges overall—electrons are neither gained nor lost—but it acquires separate regions of positive and negative charges. For example, a positively-charged rod is brought near a neutral tinsel. Because opposite charges attract, electrons within the tinsel are drawn toward that part of the tinsel closest to the rod. This leaves more protons than electrons in the region of the tinsel farthest from the acrylic rod. By using tinsel and the rod, students are able to see this phenomenon as it occurs.

Once the tinsel gets close enough to the rod, electrons from the tinsel can actually jump the gap between tinsel and rod. This gives the tinsel an overall positive charge, so it repels the rod.

PREPARATION

Have available the empty soda can, the balloon, and the other materials you will need for the *Launching the Lesson* section. Practice procedures described in the *Student Activity* section, especially step 2, beforehand.

LAUNCHING THE LESSON

Have someone place an empty soda can on a table and then charge an acrylic rod by rubbing it with the wool cloth. First have students predict what will happen when the positively-charged rod is held near the can and then have a student experiment to see what actually happens.

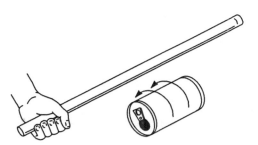

Next, have a student rub the balloon with a wool cloth. Ask for predictions about how the can will respond to the charged balloon. Then have the student try this out.

Recharge the balloon and ask what will happen when you place it near a wall. Then do so.

Finally, fly a tinsel loop and then lasso it with your finger. This provides a perfect opportunity to comment on the loop's attraction to your hand.

Draw these demonstrations together by asking what was similar about all of them. If necessary, help students to realize that each one involved attraction between a charged object and a neutral object.

Challenge students to develop an explanation for why a neutral object is attracted to a charged object. The following activity will help them to discover an answer.

STUDENT ACTIVITY

Have students prepare special charge testers by following steps 1-4:

1. Make two tinsel charge-testers and set them up about a meter apart. Hold them in place by books.

2. Trim the tinsel on one tinsel charge-tester so that it is a few centimeters shorter than the total length of the two straws.

3. Trim the second tinsel so that it is half the length of the first.

4. Charge an acrylic rod with a wool cloth and then charge the *short* tinsel with the rod. What charges do the rod and the tinsel have? (Students should respond that both the tinsel and the rod have positive charges.)

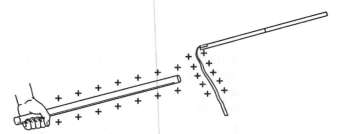

5. Hold the rod just above the long tinsel, close enough to make only the top of the tinsel bend toward the rod. This may take some practice.

6. One person should keep holding the rod above the long tinsel while another brings the short tinsel near the bottom half of the long tinsel.

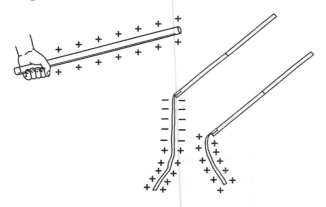

Ask students why the bottom half of the long tinsel repels the short tinsel. Students should conclude that the bottom half of the tinsel is positively charged. (Only a positive charge can repel a positive charge.)

7. Remove the short tinsel and *then* remove the charged rod from the top of the long tinsel. Test the long tinsel by offering it your finger. If you have worked carefully, your tinsel should *not* be attracted. This shows that even though the bottom of it was positively charged, the tinsel gained no charge overall.

Now, redirect students' experiments by asking whether it is possible to use a positively-charged rod to give a tinsel a negative charge. Then have students proceed through steps 8-11.

8. Charge a short tinsel with the balloon.

9. Hold a charged rod near the bottom of the long tinsel.

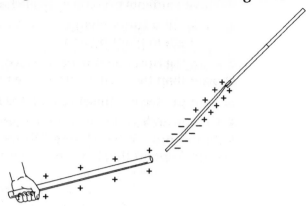

Be careful not to let the rod get too close or some of its charge will transfer to the tinsel. (You will know this happens if you hear a crackling sound or if the tinsel is repelled. If either of these events occurs, ground the tinsel and start again.)

10. One person should keep holding the rod while another touches the middle of the tinsel with a finger and then removes the finger.

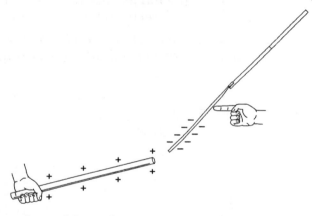

Now remove the rod from the tinsel.

11. Test the long tinsel by bringing the short, negatively-charged tinsel near it. What happens? (The two tinsels should repel, indicating that *the long tinsel acquired a negative charge from a positive rod.*)

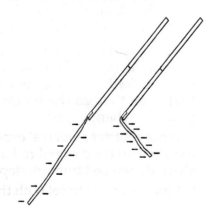

Troubleshooting

Here are some problems students may encounter:

• *In step 3, the long tinsel may have become charged by the rod.* If so, have students either hold the rod farther away from the tinsel or charge the rod less by rubbing it only lightly.

• *In step 7, the long tinsel may gain a positive charge from the rod.* Students should hold the rod farther away from the long tinsel. If they hear the telltale crackling sound of a charge transferring, they need to ground the tinsel and start again, this time keeping the rod even farther away.

• *The long tinsel may gain no charge at all.* Students are not keeping the charged rod in place near the tinsel before, during, and after touching the tinsel. Make sure they remove a finger from the tinsel before removing the rod.

MAKING CONNECTIONS

Copy the following statements on the chalkboard:

• Neutral is a mix of positive and negative charges.

• Like charges repel.

• Opposites attract.

Ask students to use these statements to explain what happened in steps 5 and 6. Here are some actual explanations suggested by fifth and sixth graders: The long, neutral tinsel has both positive and negative charges within it. Because opposites attract, the negative charges are attracted by the positive acrylic rod. For this reason, the negative charges move up toward the top of the tinsel. Because like charges repel, the bottom half of the tinsel acquires a positive charge. Now that the bottom of the tinsel is positively charged, it repels the positively charged short tinsel.

For steps 9-11 students explained that negative charges already present in the neutral tinsel are attracted to the rod. The negative charges crowd into the end of the tinsel closest to the rod, leaving a positive charge in the rest of the tinsel; overall, however, the tinsel remains neutral. Touching the tinsel grounds the negative charge so that all but the negative end of the tinsel becomes neutral. When the acrylic rod is removed, the negative charges in the bottom of the tinsel spread out, since like charges repel. This gives the tinsel an overall negative charge.

Tell students that this process is called *electrostatic induction*, which means the "imbalancing of charges." Ask them to explain in their own words what "the imbalancing of charges" means and exactly what happened with the can and the balloon in the *Launching the Activity* section.

FOR FURTHER INVESTIGATION

Here is another interesting example of electrostatic induction at work. Write directions for the activity on the chalkboard so that students can pursue it on their own:

• Bend a thin stream of water from a faucet by holding a charged object nearby. Record what happens and try to explain why.

·7· *Tiny Shocks*

A Pie-tin Electrophorus

Time **One period**

MATERIALS
For each small group of students:

1 acrylic plate about 8" x 8" and of any thickness

1 aluminum pie tin with flat bottom and no design (or 1 phonograph record with label removed, or polycarbonate plate, or various plastic containers, or some foam-plastic plates)*

1 plastic pen (or 1 plastic straw, rubber bands, styrofoam, or pencil)*

1 thumbtack (or 1 brass fastener)*

1 hot melt glue gun and glue sticks (or regular white glue)*

4 plastic straws (or plastic pens or rulers)

1 acrylic rod (or 1 acrylic plate)

1 inflated balloon (or 1 negative charge source)

1 wool cloth (or 1 silk cloth)

2 tinsel strands (or 1 aluminum or copper sheet)

*For teacher also

OVERVIEW
The purpose of this lesson is to introduce the *electrophorus, (e-lek-trah-for-us)*, which will serve as the charge engine for the rest of this lesson. Each small group of students builds a pie-tin electrophorus, which can repeatedly produce a tiny blue spark that students can see and hear. It also produces a slight shock.

TEACHER BACKGROUND
The electrophorus, Latin for "charge carrier," delivers a small shock on demand. It is similar to the one you get by scuffling your shoes across a carpet on a dry winter day.

The electrophorus consists of an acrylic plate and a pie tin with an insulated handle made from an object such as a pen. To charge the electrophorus, the acrylic plate must first be rubbed with a wool cloth, thereby giving it a positive charge. The pie tin is then held by its handle and lowered onto the acrylic plate. Through this process, two regions of charge (positive on top, negative below) are induced within the pie tin. This parallels the induction of charges in the long tinsel in the *Student Activity* section of Lesson 6.

Next, the user touches the top of the pie tin, thereby grounding the positive charge. When the pie tin is then picked up by its insulated handle, it has only a negative charge.

At this point, when the pie tin is touched, it gives a small shock. The shock is produced by the negative charges escaping from the pie tin. The pie tin can be recharged simply by lowering it back down onto the acrylic plate, grounding it, and picking it up again. Curiously, the acrylic plate does not need to be recharged.

Students will undertake a more detailed investigation of the electrophorus in Lesson 9, *A Second Look*.

Note: See suggestions after the Making Connections *section for making an electrophorus from substitute materials.*

PREPARATION

Following the instructions in the *Student Activity* section, construct one electrophorus for demonstration purposes. Practice charging and discharging it until you are proficient.

LAUNCHING THE LESSON

As students watch, charge your electrophorus. Then make the room as dark as possible. Ask for a volunteer to come to the front of the room: Shock his or her finger. Students should be able to hear the snap of the pie tin discharging. Some will even see the thin blue "lightning bolt." Students will probably clamor to try this themselves—indulge them. If they play with the electrophorus now, students will learn to operate it proficiently before they construct their own.

Before the *Student Activity* section, when each group of students makes and uses an electrophorus, announce the following rule:

Do not shock anyone unless he or she is prepared for it, and has agreed to be shocked.

Every student should agree to follow this rule before proceeding.

STUDENT ACTIVITY

These are the steps for constructing the electrophorus:

1. Push a thumbtack carefully up through the middle of an aluminum pie tin.

2. To make a handle, remove the ink cartridge from a plastic pen. Put a glob of hot melted glue over the point of the thumbtack and push the pen shaft on to it. (Students may require your assistance with this step.)

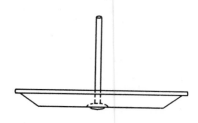

3. Put the pie tin on a table and allow it to cool for about five minutes.

Now offer these directions for using the electrophorus:

4. Rub the acrylic plate vigorously with a wool cloth.

5. Hold the pie tin by its handle and place it down on top of the charged acrylic plate.

6. Touch the top of the pie tin. (Students may feel a small shock.)

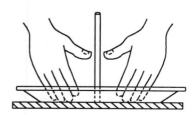

7. Remove your hands from the pie tin and then pick it up by its handle.

8. Bring a finger or knuckle slowly to the pie tin and feel the small shock.

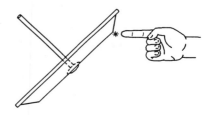

9. Recharge the pie tin by placing it back down on the acrylic plate. You don't need to rub the acrylic plate again because its charge hasn't been used up.

10. Now use four straws and two tinsels to make two tinsel charge testers. Use these to tell whether the pie tin gains a positive or negative charge. (Mention that the only proof you will accept will be repulsion between two objects.)

Circulate among the groups. Ask students to explain their strategies. Offer suggestions as needed. Using tinsel and an acrylic rod, students should be able to show that the acrylic plate has a positive charge. Some students may suggest that the acrylic plate and rod are made of the same thing and must, therefore, have the same charge.

Students should also be able to use a tinsel and a balloon to show that the pie tin has acquired a negative charge. This may come as a surprise to many of them. (Students may attempt to use the attraction between the pie tin and a tinsel charged by the acrylic rod. Don't accept this as ultimate proof that the pie tin has a negative charge; insist that students use repulsion to identify the charge on the pie tin.)

Troubleshooting

If a group's electrophorus won't charge, look for the following:

• *The acrylic plate is not adequately charged.* Students should rub the acrylic plate again with the wool cloth, using long, firm strokes.

• *The wool cloth is damp from handling.* Students must not hold the wool cloth between rubbing.

• *The acrylic plate is adequately charged, but the pie tin will not shock.* A student may have become charged and is no longer an effective ground. If so, he or she should remove his or her shoes and touch a metal chair or table leg with a stocking foot. The student will regain the ability to ground and then charge the electrophorus. If the problem is that the pen has become a conductor, another pen should be substituted.

MAKING CONNECTIONS

Remind students of the previous lesson in which a positive rod was used to give a piece of tinsel a negative charge. Perhaps this reminder will be all some students will need to explain how the electrophorus is charged and shocked. More discussion of this process will follow in Lesson 9. For now, here are some intriguing questions concerning the electrophorus that students may want to discuss or add to their wall chart of questions:

• *Why does the electrophorus shock?*

• *Why does the electrophorus shock only once?* (After it shocks, it becomes neutral. The shocking itself occurs when the positively-charged pie tin draws needed electrons from whatever it touches.)

• *Why must you touch the pie tin before you lift it from the plate? What happens if you don't?*

• *How can the electrophorus shock over and over again if you don't rub the acrylic plate each time?*

FOR FURTHER INVESTIGATION

Students can make an electrophorus with the substitute materials shown below:

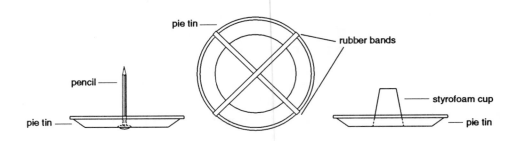

The whole class can try some of the following activities together:

• Discharge the electrophorus through a small neon bulb. You will see a momentary glow between the bulb's electrodes. Hold on to one of the bulb's legs, and touch the charged pie tin to the other leg.

• Investigate the pie tin's repellent charge. After you have grounded the pie tin, but before you pick it up, sprinkle on cut-up pieces of tinsel or paper confetti. When you lift the pie tin by its handle, the tinsel will jump off.

• Fly some tinsel. Use the pie tin in place of the acrylic rod to fly a loop of tinsel, as you did in Lesson 1.

HISTORY

In the eighteenth century, the most common source of electric charge was a sulphur or glass globe spun with one hand and touched with the other. Although effective, it was cumbersome and expensive. Eventually, Alessandro Volta, after whom the volt is named, invented the electrophorus. It was considered a small, inexpensive, and easy way to produce an electric charge.

·8·

A Big Shock

The Milk-jug Leyden Jar

Time **One period**

MATERIALS
For each small group of students:

2 12" x 12" aluminum foil strips*

1 1-gallon plastic milk jug* (or high density polyethylene sheeting or any plastic container made of high-density polyethylene—usually designated with a "2" in a triangle of three arrows—or plastic grocery or garbage bags)

2 test leads* (or strips of aluminum foil and masking tape)

1 roll of Scotch tape* (or any kind of cellophane or electrical tape)

1 wool cloth (or 1 silk cloth)

1 container of rubber cement or glue*

1 scissors*

1 electrophorus

*For teacher also

OVERVIEW
Students will study the workings of the Leyden jar, or capacitor, a device for storing electricity. They will construct Leyden jars from disposable plastic milk jugs and use their electrophori to charge them. Students will then have an opportunity to experience the small shock that their Leyden jars deliver.

TEACHER BACKGROUND
Please read the *History* section before continuing. What was originally called the Leyden jar is now very well known as the capacitor—an essential and ubiquitous component in electronic devices. It is worth making and studying capacitors for many reasons. The capacitor becomes an effective investigative tool in subsequent lessons. Because the capacitor produces a momentary flow of charge through a wire, the activity provides a natural lead into the study of current electricity. Most of all, students find working with the capacitor an extremely engrossing activity.

If you have never experienced it before, you may be surprised at the strength with which the capacitor can shock after having been charged just a few times with an electrophorus. The sensation of the shock delivered by the capacitor is greater than that of the electrophorus for two reasons. First, the capacitor allows larger charges to build up between shocks—it essentially accumulates the many charges from the electrophorus. Second, the charge is directed to flow through you. Electrons deposited on the top foil of the capacitor travel through your hand on their way to the strong positive charge on the bottom of the capacitor. In contrast, when the electrophorus shocks you, its charge spreads out through your body. As the charge spreads out, the intensity of the shock dissipates.

CAUTION

It is recommended that you follow the prescribed safety procedure given in the *Student Activity* section. This procedure is designed so that students can feel the shock safely. Despite the extra care you must take, the capacitor shock is such an extraordinary demonstration that it is worth the effort. Before inviting your students to try it, please make your own capacitor and sample the shock for yourself.

PREPARATION

Construct your own milk-jug capacitor, following the steps in the *Student Activity* section. Practice charging and discharging it until you can do so reliably. Prior to the lesson, remind students to wear rubber-soled shoes for this experiment.

LAUNCHING THE LESSON

Set up your capacitor. Tell the Leyden-jar story from the *History* section while charging the capacitor with the electrophorus. Charge it about 20 times. Stop the story just as Cunaeus is about to get his big shock. Invite three students who are wearing rubber-soled shoes to come up and feel what Cunaeus felt. *But first read and emphasize the safety procedures described in the* Student Activity *section*. Then and only then, have students link right thumbs. Let students feel the shock. They may be surprised at its strength, which should be felt in each student's right hand only.

Afterwards, finish telling students the Leyden-jar story. Tell students that they will make their own Leyden jars, or capacitors, and learn to charge and discharge them safely. Each small group of students can make one capacitor.

STUDENT ACTIVITY

Direct students to remove the label from a gallon milk jug, cut the jug in half and clean and dry it. Next, give students the following directions:
1. Cut two pieces of aluminum foil to fit the bottom of the jug. Glue one piece of foil to the inside and another to the outside bottom. Smooth each piece of foil down so that it makes complete contact with the milk jug. (The more ridges in the foil, the less effective the capacitor will be.)

Note: If students use rubber cement, be sure to provide for adequate ventilation.

2. Tear off two strips of foil, each about 2 centimeters wide. Tape (don't glue) one strip of the foil on the outside of the milk jug. The strip should extend from the middle of the jug to about 2 centimeters beyond the jug's edge. Tape the other foil strip to the inner foil layer so that it extends

from the middle, up one side, and a few centimeters over the top edge of the milk jug.

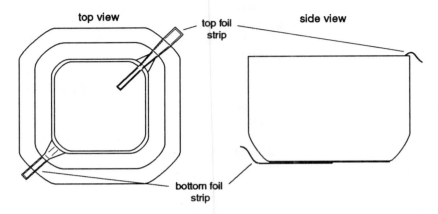

top view   top foil strip   side view

bottom foil strip

Before allowing students to continue, repeat the safety procedures given below. Have each student agree to follow them before you begin.

SAFETY PROCEDURES
- Keep one hand behind your back or in a pocket at all times when charging or discharging the capacitor.
- Always wear rubber-soled shoes.
- Never charge or discharge the capacitor if you are wet or perspiring.
- Feel the shock with one hand only.

---

3. Connect one end of a test lead, or a homemade aluminum wire, to the foil strip on the outside bottom layer of aluminum. Clip the other end of the test lead to a large metal "ground." Good grounds in the classroom include filing cabinets (clip the test lead onto an unpainted portion), water-faucet handles, metal chair or desk legs, and aluminum chalkboard frames.

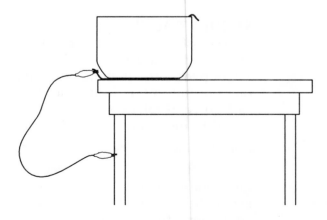

4. Charge an electrophorus and deliver the charge to the foil strip connected to the inside (top) foil layer. You may or may not hear a snap.

Allow students to continue charging the capacitor a total of 20 times with the electrophorus.

CAUTION

Do not have students touch the top layer of the capacitor and the ground at the same time, or they may get a shock before they are ready for it.

Instruct students to carry out steps 5-7. *Continue to monitor students to make sure that the safety procedures are followed.*

5. Disconnect the alligator clip from the ground, leaving the other alligator clip on the outer (bottom) foil layer. Touch the alligator clip to the inside (top) foil layer. You will hear a "snap."

6. Recharge the capacitor. Once charged, detach the alligator clip from the ground but keep the test lead attached to the outer (bottom) foil layer. (Repeat the safety procedures.) For one student to feel the shock, he or she should grab the free alligator clip between two fingers of one hand and then touch the bottom foil layer with another finger from the same hand.

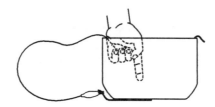

7. Recharge the capacitor once again. Then make a chain of up to five students to discharge the capacitor. Everyone should put one right-hand thumb into the chain. Be sure to keep one hand behind your back. The first person in the chain should hold the alligator clip while the last person touches the top of the capacitor.

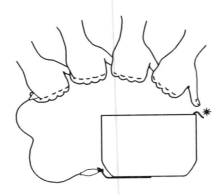

CAUTION

Do not, under any circumstances, allow students to use anything but the electrophorus to charge the capacitor. **Do not allow them to use household current. Do not use Van de Graaf or Wimhurst generators to charge the capacitor.**

MAKING CONNECTIONS

This activity naturally raises many questions, including these:

- *Why does the capacitor shock harder than the electrophorus?*
- *Why must the capacitor be grounded to be most effective?*
- *Why do you feel the shock through your entire hand?*

Students may be inspired to ask more "why" questions. The best response, at this point, is to tell students that during the next lesson they will have a chance to discover answers.

FOR FURTHER INVESTIGATION

Supervise student groups as they experiment with the following activities:

• Charge and discharge the capacitor without the grounding wire. See whether it will deliver as strong a shock as it did with a wire attached to the "ground." Decide why it does or does not.

• Dismantle a modern ceramic capacitor. It is easy to recognize the two foil pieces of the capacitor. You can find these at any electronics store.

HISTORY

One discovery above all others triggered an avalanche of interest in electricity. The Leyden jar, as it came to be known, was discovered by accident in 1745 in Leyden, Holland, when Dr. Pieter van Musschenbroek and his assistant, Cunaeus, attempted to collect electric "fluid" in a jar of water.

The two men had run a metal chain from a large charge-producing machine into the water in the jug. Cunaeus held the jar steady with his hand. Because his hand was wet, water was deposited on the outside of the jar. Now the jar had water both inside and outside.

The charge machine ran for a long time, but no electric fluid seemed to accumulate. Disappointed, Cunaeus attempted to unhook the apparatus. Still holding the jar with one hand, he touched the chain with the other hand. At the moment he touched it, he received a violent shock.

Dr. Musschenbroek described his experiment in detail in a letter to scientific colleagues in France. He cautioned them never to repeat the jar experiment, warning that its shock was simply too dangerous. Of course, such a warning had the opposite effect of that intended. Soon, experimenters throughout Europe and America were building their own Leyden jars, and a new era of electrical experimentation began. The Leyden jar survives to this day as the capacitor— an essential component in almost every electronic device.

·9·

A Second Look

The Electrophorus and the Leyden Jar

Time **One period**

MATERIALS

In this activity, students will work in just two groups, and their needs will vary, depending upon the experiments they decide to do. The following are some of the materials students may request:

milk-jug Leyden jars

test leads (or aluminum foil and masking tape)

electrophori

straws

tinsel

acrylic plates

balloons (or other negative sources, as identified in Lesson 4)

acrylic rods (or other positive sources, as identified in Lesson 4)

wool cloth (or silk cloth)

OVERVIEW

You and your students will discuss the atom, with its positively charged protons and its negatively charged electrons. Students will then go on to design experiments for investigating negative charges with the electrophorus and the capacitor.

TEACHER BACKGROUND

It is fascinating that the results of simple experiments such as those recreated in the first five lessons led to concepts that remain valid to this day. We still believe, as Benjamin Franklin did, that there are two kinds of electric charges: positive and negative. Today, however, we know that the charges reside in the protons and electrons of the atom. We still make wide use of the basic relationships between charges: like charges repel, opposites attract, and objects containing an equal number of positive and negative charges are neutral. These concepts are used to explain all manner of electrical phenomena.

PREPARATION

Read over the information in the *Launching the Lesson* section. Think about the special needs of your students, what they have gleaned from the lessons so far, and how you might stimulate and guide them to think logically, to comment, and to ask good questions.

On the chalkboard, write the questions that students will consider when they come to the *Student Activity* section of this lesson.

LAUNCHING THE LESSON

Introduce the concept of the atom by quickly sketching on the chalkboard the diagram of the atom shown below.

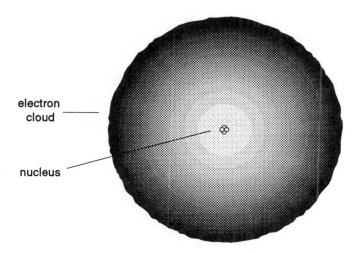

electron cloud

nucleus

Choose some or all of the following information to discuss with students:

• All matter is made of atoms. A sheet of paper is much more than a million atoms thick.

• Each atom has a nucleus made up of neutrons, which are neutral, protons, which are positively charged, and electrons, which are lighter than neutrons and protons and are negatively charged.

• Electrons can jump from the atoms of one object to those of another object. Protons cannot move.

• When a neutral, or uncharged, acrylic rod is rubbed with a wool cloth, some of the rod's electrons jump to the cloth. The rod is no longer neutral. Because it is left with fewer electrons and a greater number of protons, the rod is now positively charged.

• When a balloon is rubbed with a wool cloth, electrons jump from the cloth to the balloon. The balloon now has a greater number of electrons and is negatively charged.

Ask volunteers to use a rod, a balloon, and a wool cloth to demonstrate what has been discussed. As they demonstrate, have students refer to the atom diagram to explain what is happening.

Ask students to use this new information to explain the concepts *like charges repel, opposite charges attract,* and *an even mix of positive and negative charges creates a neutral object.*

This is a good time for students to look again at the questions they have been recording on the wall chart to see if more of them can be answered now. Tell students that they should keep the information just discussed in mind as they investigate to explain how the electrophorus and capacitor actually work.

STUDENT ACTIVITY

Divide the class into two investigatory units. Challenge student groups within the first unit to investigate and explain how the electrophorus becomes charged and discharged. Assign the other unit to investigate the capacitor. Direct each group's attention to the questions to be answered.

Have these questions for each group available on the chalkboard:

Investigating the Electrophorus

1. When you rub the acrylic plate with a wool cloth, does it become positively or negatively charged? How do you know?

2. How does the pie tin becomes charged?

3. Why doesn't the charge on the acrylic plate get "used up?"

4. At the end, why do the pie tin and the acrylic plate have opposite charges?

Investigating the Leyden Jar

1. Is the plastic middle of the capacitor a conductor? Can an electric charge pass through it?

2. What are the charges on the top and bottom of a charged capacitor?

3. What does the ground wire do?

Allow students as much freedom as possible to plan their own investigations. Let them decide on the materials they need. If students need help, suggest that they use equipment and ideas from Lessons 4 and 5. Tinsel charge-testers made from tinsel and plastic straws are useful for testing the presence of electric charges. They also help test the concepts that like charges repel and opposite charges attract. Students may also find their lists of charged objects useful.

MAKING CONNECTIONS

Have students report their findings to the class. Guide the class toward a complete understanding of how the electrophorus and the capacitor work. With a good deal of encouragement and artful questioning from you, students often can come up with these explanations on their own. Through discussion, the following information should emerge:

• *How the pie tin is charged.* Recall that the acrylic plate has a positive charge and that, at first, the pie tin is neutral. When the pie tin is laid upon the acrylic, some of the electrons within the pie tin are drawn down toward the acrylic's positive charge. The top of the pie tin is left with more protons than electrons, so the top has an overall positive charge, as in the illustration on the left below.

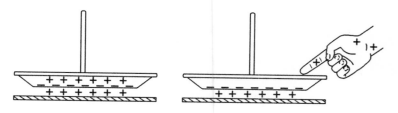

When you touch the pie tin, as shown in the picture on the previous page on the right, you ground, or neutralize, the positive charge on top. In other words, electrons are pulled from your body into the top of the pie tin (because opposite charges attract). All the while, the bottom of the pie tin remains negatively charged, for the electrons are held in place by the attraction to the positively-charged acrylic. When you pick up the pie tin, these negative charges (electrons) spread out. Thus the pie tin acquires a negative charge from a positively charged piece of acrylic.

• *How the pie tin shocks.* The pie tin shocks you by pushing electrons into you. It only shocks once because it gets rid of all the extra electrons it needs to the first time. Then, having rid itself of extra electrons, it becomes neutral—a balance of positive and negative charges.

• *Why the pie tin and the acrylic plate have opposite charges.* This is easy to demonstrate with a simple experiment. If you charge a tinsel positively with an acrylic rod, or other standard positive charge, you can show that it repels the acrylic plate. If you charge another tinsel negatively, with a balloon or other negative charge source, you can show that the charged pie tin repels the negative tinsel.

• *How the electrophorus charges the capacitor.* Each time the negatively-charged pie tin touches the top foil of the capacitor, it deposits extra electrons on the foil. More and more electrons are placed on the foil with each additional application, so the top foil layer gains a strong negative charge.

• *What the bottom layer of foil does.* Because of the large negative charge building up only millimeters away, electrons are repelled from the bottom foil and travel through the wire into the ground. (Like charges repel.)

• *What the plastic does.* The plastic between the foils won't let the electrons on the top of the plastic pass directly through to the bottom of the plastic. Because the plastic is thin, however, the attractive force between the negative top layer and the positive bottom layer become quite strong. (If you try to peel apart a charged capacitor made of flat plastic sheets, you will feel that attractive force.)

• *What the ground does.* The ground acts as a source of atoms, which are spread by the electrons that were repelled from the bottom of the capacitor. With the ground attached, a much stronger positive charge can accumulate on the bottom of the capacitor.

• *What happens when the capacitor is discharged.* Many extra electrons in the top of the capacitor are attracted to the positively charged bottom of the capacitor. The electrons actually push through the wire to get from bottom to top, or through the body, thus causing the shock one feels.

FOR FURTHER INVESTIGATION

Challenge students to work on their own by giving them the following directive:

• Design an experiment to prove that the inner and outer (or top and bottom) sides of the capacitor have opposite charges.

If necessary, suggest that students use the equipment described in Lesson 4. Students might also find it easier to use a capacitor made out of flat pieces of polyethylene plastic instead of a milk jug.

·10· *The Tinsel Whip*

An Electrophorus Trick

Time **Thirty minutes or less**

MATERIALS
For each student or small group of students:

1 electrophorus* (or materials in Lesson 7)

2 plastic straws* (or 1 acrylic rod, 2 or 3 plastic pens connected together, plastic ruler, or plastic spatula)

1 tinsel strand* (or string with a small ball of aluminum foil or soda-can pulltab on the end)

1 small piece of masking tape* (or tape of any kind)

1 wool cloth (or 1 silk cloth)

*For teacher also

OVERVIEW
Students will make a tinsel strand whip back and forth between an electrophorus and a hand. Why does the tinsel whip back and forth with such fury? To answer this question, students will need to use everything they have learned about attraction, repulsion, and the imbalancing of charges.

TEACHER BACKGROUND
The tinsel attracts because the charges within it are imbalanced and because opposites attract. The tinsel pushes away because like charges repel. Since the charged tinsel pulls electrons from the hand, it regains neutrality and starts the cycle over again.

PREPARATION
Set up one tinsel charge-tester as shown in Lesson 3, but this time call it a tinsel whip. Also, have one electrophorus ready to use with the tinsel whip in an initial demonstration. Practice the demonstration before showing it to your class. Just before the session begins, write on the chalkboard, "Can you explain why the tinsel whips?"

LAUNCHING THE LESSON
A good way to start this lesson is to demonstrate it without words. Silently, charge the electrophorus and show how the tinsel whips back and forth. Once students see this, they will no doubt want to try it themselves. But before you have them start, direct their attention to the question on the chalkboard.

STUDENT ACTIVITY

Have students, working alone or in small groups, follow these steps:

1. Attach two straws and the tinsel together, as you did when you made the charge tester in Lesson 3. Cut the tinsel so that it is between 6 inches and 8 inches long.

2. Charge your electrophorus.

3. Bring the charged pie tin to one side of the tinsel and a hand to the other side. The tinsel should start to whip back and forth.

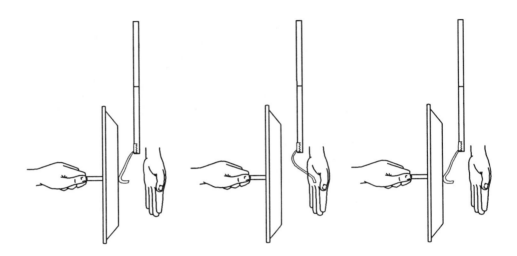

MAKING CONNECTIONS

Gather the class together and ask students to explain why the tinsel whips. In order to make the task more manageable, ask them to explain each part of the tinsel's motion separately. If necessary, use the following questions, which are followed by possible responses:

• *Why is the tinsel attracted to the pie tin?* (The neutral tinsel is attracted to the charged pie tin. The charges in the neutral tinsel separate when the charged pie tin is brought near. The pie tin has a positive charge, so it attracts the negative charges within the tinsel. The tinsel often assumes a C shape when it is attracted to the tinsel. It is likely that the middle of the C is negatively charged while both ends are positively charged, although the tinsel is still neutral overall.)

Note: It might, at this point, be useful to recall the activities and information from Lesson 6, in which charges were shown to separate.

• *Why is the tinsel repelled by the pie tin?* (The tinsel touches the positively charged pie tin and gives up some of its electrons. Thus the tinsel also assumes a positive charge. Since like charges repel, the tinsel is pushed away from the pie tin.)

• *Why is the tinsel attracted to the hand?* (A neutral object is attracted to a charged object. In this case, the neutral object is the hand, and the tinsel is positively charged. The tinsel is drawn toward the electrons in the hand. Once the tinsel touches, it takes electrons from the hand and becomes neutral again.)

• *Why does the tinsel repeat the process?* (Now that the tinsel is neutral again, it falls away from the hand. The pie tin again imbalances the tinsel's charges, creating an area of negative charge, which will be attracted to the pie tin.)

• *Why does the tinsel slow and stop?* (With every whip, the tinsel carries a load of electrons from the hand to the pie tin. Eventually, the pie tin's hunger for electrons is satisfied. When the pie tin is neutral, the tinsel stops whipping.)

FOR FURTHER INVESTIGATION
Suggest that students try the following experiment:

• Replace your hand with other objects to see if these improve the whipping action. Likely candidates include the charged acrylic plate, an uncharged pie tin, or any large metal object.

Conductors and Insulators

Using a Leyden Jar

Time **One or two periods**

MATERIALS

For each small group of students:

1 Leyden jar

2 or more test leads (or short lengths of copper wire)

1 or more electrophori (or any containers made out of paper or plastic)

various test liquids, such as salt water, vinegar, dishwashing liquid, motor oil, vaseline, vegetable oil, shortening, cola, peanut butter, honey

various solid objects such as copper, steel, other metals, wooden pencil, acrylic rod

a rubber glove*

For the whole class:

10-20 small plastic cups

1 box of paper clips

For teacher also*

OVERVIEW

Students will use their capacitors to identify conductors and insulators and will discover that the greater the capacitor's charge, the more a substance is likely to conduct.

TEACHER BACKGROUND

Conductors are substances that readily permit electrons to flow through them; insulators will not let electrons flow through. With the capacitor, many substances you might think would insulate become conductors. Students may notice that their list of insulators matches the list of charge-producing objects they compiled in Lesson 3.

The work in this lesson is especially important because of its application in the next lesson. There, students' knowledge of conductors and insulators will be one of the factors they use to determine if a voltaic pile is electric in nature. From a student's perspective, however, this experiment is appealing because it provides another opportunity for the fun of working with the electrophorus and the Leyden jar.

CAUTION

Do not use gasoline, lighter fluid, alcohol, or any other highly flammable and volatile liquid. The capacitor's spark could ignite the fumes.

PREPARATION

You will need to prepare the liquids for testing by pouring them into small cups. Depending on the number of liquids, you may want to have 2 cups of each liquid. For each cup, straighten 2 paper clips and stand them up in the liquid. These paper clips should stay with their respective liquids throughout the lesson to avoid getting more than one liquid on a paper clip, thus compromising each subsequent test. Have one rubber glove available, but out of sight, to use in the demonstration in the *Launching the Lesson* section. Look back at the results of Lesson 3 so that you are prepared when the class discusses the fifth question in the *Making Connections* section.

LAUNCHING THE LESSON

Invite two or three students to set up a capacitor and charge it 20 times. Once the capacitor is charged, point to the test lead and ask students to predict what will happen if you grab it with your hand. In all likelihood, students will expect that touching the lead will produce a shock. At this point, pull out the hidden rubber glove, quickly put it on, and grab the test lead. Students will observe that you seem not to have received any shock at all. Next, have a student do what you did and describe what he or she feels.

Of course, students will recognize that in both cases the rubber glove offered protection. Use the glove to introduce the concept of insulator—anything that will not permit the flow of electrons through it. Then tell students that the word *conductor* has just the opposite meaning; have them produce a definition for this word.

STUDENT ACTIVITY

Ask students to speculate about other objects or things that might be either insulators or conductors. Then tell students that they can use their own capacitors to identify conductors and insulators. Sketch charts on the chalkboard like the ones below and have one student from each group make similar recording sheets.

Solids		Liquids	
Conductors	Insulators	Conductors	Insulators

Direct students to gather their capacitors, one electrophorus or more, test leads, and wool cloths. Each group should also collect solid objects from around the room that they think might be conductors or insulators. Have students then work in their groups, following these directions as you give them:

1. Charge your capacitors 20 times with the electrophorus.

2. When your capacitor is charged, detach the alligator clip from the

ground and attach it to the first test object.

3. Bring the test object to the top of the capacitor, then look and listen carefully for a spark. (A spark shows that electrons have passed through the test object and that the object is a conductor.)

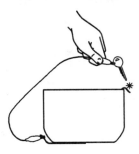

Record your findings for each object in the appropriate column on your recording sheet.

If there is no spark, the object may be an insulator. (Point out that no spark could also mean that the capacitor wasn't charged.)

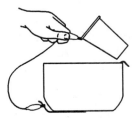

To make sure a capacitor was really charged, students should detach the test object and touch the alligator clip directly to the top of the capacitor. If they see a spark or hear a pop, they can conclude that the object is an conductor.

Make sure students understand the importance of carrying out this step before following steps 4-7.

4. Test at least 10 solid objects. Use as wide a variety of materials as possible. Remember to record your findings on your data recording sheet for solid objects.

Have one student from each group bring one liquid-filled cup with its

2 clips to the group. (Cups should be rotated so each group tests every kind of liquid.) Give the following directions:

5. Now test some liquids to see if they are conductors. Recharge the capacitor and attach one wire from the bottom of the capacitor to one of the paper clips in the liquid. Attach the other wire to the other paper clip. *Be careful not to let the paper clips within each cup touch each other so that the electrons will have to flow through some of the liquid.*

6. Bring the free alligator clip to the top of the capacitor and observe the reaction. If there is a pop and a spark, which indicates that electrons have flowed, the liquid is a conductor.

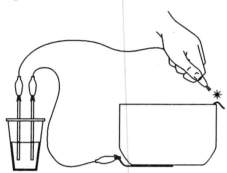

If there is no spark or pop, the liquid may be an insulator. But first students must make sure that the capacitor was really charged. Have them remove the test liquid and attempt to discharge the capacitor directly through the wires. If they hear a pop or see a spark now, the liquid was an insulator. If they hear no pop or spark, they can conclude that the capacitor was not adequately charged.

7. Now test other liquids and record your findings.

MAKING CONNECTIONS

Use questions such as the following to focus attention on some interesting aspects of the experiment students just completed:

• *Do you notice any patterns among the solid conductors and insulators?* (Perceptive students may note that the previously identified charge-producing objects all seem to be insulators.)

• *Why do we have to perform a second step—direct discharge of the capacitor—to positively identify an insulator?* (Students should mention that we must make sure the capacitor was charged to begin with; perhaps the object was an insulator, but the Leyden jar wasn't charged.)

• *Do you notice any similarities or patterns among the conducting or insulating liquids?*

• *Why is it important to keep the two paper clips from touching in the test liquid?* (If students don't know, tell them that electrons must be forced to flow through the liquid being tested. If the paper clips touch, the electrons will flow directly from one paper clip to another, bypassing the liquid entirely.)

• *Is there any correlation between the lists made in Lesson 3 and the lists you made today?* (Help students see that the objects identified as charge producers are good insulators.)

• *Can this help you explain why you can't rub a conductor with wool and produce a noticeable charge?* (Although a charge is probably produced, it is immediately grounded because the conductor is being held. With an insulator such as an acrylic rod, any charge that is produced stays on the surface.)

FOR FURTHER INVESTIGATION

There is so much more that can be done with conductors, insulators, and capacitors. As time allows, have your students pursue the following ideas:

• Determine if air is a conductor or an insulator.

• Bring in liquids from home that may be insulators. Test them.

CAUTION

Do not let students work with volatile or flammable materials. The capacitor produces sparks that could ignite substances such as alcohol or gasoline.

• Attempt to find semiconductors—in this case, liquids that allow some of the charge to pass through but leave the capacitor partially charged. Peanut butter, honey, motor oil, and olive oil are good examples.

HISTORY

The large shock of the Leyden jar was so intriguing that it focused a tremendous amount of attention on the study of electricity, which eventually led to a deepening understanding of the subject. Conductors and insulators were classified well before the first battery, light bulb, or multimeter was invented.

·12· Quick as a Wink

Investigating the Speed of Electricity

Time **One period**

MATERIALS
For each small group of students:

1 Leyden jar*

1 electrophorus*

1 wool cloth (or silk cloth or piece of fur)

4 test leads*

1 long insulated wire (20' to 50' or even longer), with ends stripped*

2 small neon bulbs*

1 roll masking tape (or any tape)*

*For teacher also

OVERVIEW
Students will use capacitors and neon bulbs to investigate the speed of the flow of an electric charge through a wire. Students will attempt to gauge the speed of an electron flow but without the group shock. This is an experiment with a negative result in the sense that students will not be able to measure the current's speed. But part of the value of the experiment is that it can show students that they can learn from an experiment that doesn't work.

TEACHER BACKGROUND
See the *History* section for an anecdote you will need to retell in the *Launching the Lesson* section.

PREPARATION
Assemble a model of the experiment outlined in the *Student Activity* section. It will help students considerably to see one preconstructed.

LAUNCHING THE LESSON
The "monk" story recounted in the *History* section is a good introduction to this lesson. Tell the story but stop before you get to the end. Explain that the class will also try this experiment today. You might add that, unfortunately, you were unable to arrange for the transportation of 1,000 monks, so students will have to make do with neon bulbs and wires instead.

Show students how you have set up the experiment. Explain that when the capacitor is discharged through the wires, the electrons will have to pass through one neon bulb on the way "out" into the long wire, which will make the neon bulb flash. Then the electrons will travel through the wire and jump through the other neon bulb on their way "in" to the capacitor.

Point out that if the electrons were to travel very slowly, students would see the first spark, experience a long wait as the electrons traveled through the long wire, then see the second spark. If the electrons were to move faster, the time between sparks would be shorter because it would take less time to travel through the long wire. If the electrons were to travel fast enough, students might seem to see both sparks at the same time. Before proceeding with the activity, remind students of the safety procedures concerning the capacitors.

SAFETY PROCEDURES
- Keep one hand behind your back or in a pocket at all times when charging or discharging the capacitor.
- Always wear rubber-soled shoes.
- Never charge or discharge the capacitor if you are wet or perspiring.
- Don't discharge the capacitor with two hands. Feel the shock with one hand only.

STUDENT ACTIVITY
Give students the following instructions:

1. Tape two neon bulbs side by side on a tabletop and connect test leads to each "leg" of the bulbs. One of these test leads should also be attached to the bottom of the capacitor.

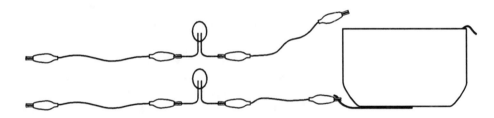

2. Stretch out the long wire and attach it to the two test leads (as shown on page 58).

3. Give the capacitor a good charge with about 20 applications of the electrophorus.

4. One person in each group, *observing safety precautions*, should touch the free test lead to the top of the capacitor. The other group members

should look for the flashes of light in the neon bulbs, as shown in the following illustration.

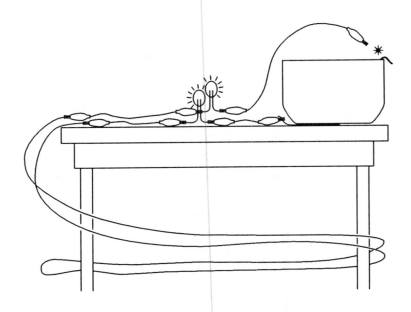

MAKING CONNECTIONS

Tell the ending of the monk story—all of the monks jumped at once. Ask how this corresponds with what your students found. Most will realize that they saw the two neon bulbs flash at the same time.

Ask students to respond to these questions:

• *What can you conclude about how fast electrons flow from the bottom layer of the capacitor to the top?* (Students will probably state that the electrons move too fast to be measured.)

• *Can you think of any practical ways that we take advantage of the electron flow's amazing speed?* (Someone might suggest that telephones and telegraphs use the nearly instantaneous speed of electricity through wires for long-distance communication.)

FOR FURTHER INVESTIGATION

Ask students whether they have ever wondered if some kinds of conductors, semiconductors, or insulators might slow down the electron flow. Then have students do the following activity:

• Design a system that would send electrons through a semiconductor, such as peanut butter, as well as through the long wire. Try to use the flashers in the neon bulbs to judge the speed. Notice whether there are any differences between these results and what happened in your previous experiment.

HISTORY

One of the first men to experiment extensively with the Leyden jar was a high church official in France named Abbe Nollet. He wondered how fast an electric charge could be made to flow. Legend holds that Nollet used the power of his political station to coerce hundreds of monks into forming a huge human ring. He then discharged a series of large Leyden jars, sending the electrons through the men. Nollet expected to see the monks jump one at a time as the charge passed from man to man on its way around the circle. Instead, to his astonishment, everyone seemed to jump at once. From this experience, Nollet concluded that an electric charge travels extraordinarily quickly.

UNIT ·2·

Current Electricity

This unit retraces an important period of scientific discovery, from Volta's introduction of the pile to the formulation of Ohm's law. The most important concepts presented are *voltage, current,* and *resistance.*

It is difficult for many students to begin to understand these concepts when they are given only textbook definitions and lack any direct experience with them. Here, we attempt to give students an opportunity to grasp these concepts intuitively by providing sensory experiences that involve touching, smelling, seeing, and even hearing.

Students are led to think of voltage as the shocking potential of a voltaic pile and then, in later lessons, to refine their definition to the push on the electrons in a circuit. At the same time, students come to see that current is a measure of how much electricity flows in a circuit at a given moment. Thus, students can begin to realize that voltage is the push on electrons and that current is the amount of electrons that flow.

By feeling the heat produced in various circuits, students explore resistance. As a result, they learn that cells connected in series and parallel influence how much total resistance a circuit has. Students learn also that current is affected by resistance—the less resistance, the greater the current.

Ohm's law, which relates voltage, current, and resistance, is introduced with the squeeze-bottle model. The water flowing out of the bottle represents current. The nozzle, which slides from open to closed, represents resistance. Voltage is represented by the push on the side of the bottle. It is easy for students to see that pushing harder increases the flow of water and that opening the nozzle increases the flow of water. This translates to the realization that increasing the voltage increases the current in a circuit and that decreasing the resistance increases the current in a circuit. This corresponds to the equation $I=E/R$, where I is the current, E is the voltage, and R is the resistance.

Students make a number of other discoveries along the way. Electrolysis demonstrates that the flow of current is continuous—students are able to see a constant stream of bubbles forming at the electrodes. Students also see that electricity is related to chemistry, for electrolysis produces chemical compounds not present beforehand, and chemical reactions are evident within the voltaic pile. Students also gather evidence indicating that current electricity (once called galvanic or voltaic electricity, after Galvani and Volta, respectively) has many of the same properties as static electricity.

? >
·13· A New Shock

Recreating the First Battery

Time **One period**

MATERIALS

For the entire class:

20 zinc plates 7.5 cm square

20 copper plates 10 cm square (or 10-20 new AA-cells—use heavy-duty variety and avoid alkaline cells)

20 paper towels

1 quart of white vinegar (or 2 quarts saturated salt water)

1 cup of water

¼ cup of salt

5-6 cups, 10 ounces or larger (or any container 10 ounces or larger)

4 2-liter soda bottles filled with water

1 sheet of aluminum foil 1' by 2'

2 test leads

1 heavy paperweight (or any heavy nonconducting material to hold pile upright)

OVERVIEW

Students will recreate the world's first battery by building one 2-layer voltaic pile and feeling its moderately shocking force. This experience provides an opportunity for students to begin understanding the concept of voltage. Students will learn that each cell delivers approximately one volt (actually, 1.1 volts). They will also observe that the number of volts seems to be a measure of how hard the pile can shock.

The concept of voltage will continue to be refined as students progress through the lesson. Ultimately, they will recognize that voltage is a measure of how hard the electrons are being pushed in a circuit.

TEACHER BACKGROUND

Please read the *History* section. Students will notice that the nature of the shock from the voltaic pile is less easily felt than that from the capacitor. In fact, they will need to lower their skin's resistance by soaking their fingers in salt water if they are to feel the shock at all.

Many published descriptions of the voltaic pile are inaccurate. Please be sure to follow the directions in the *Student Activity* section carefully.

There is a small added benefit that comes with this historical lesson: The symbol that scientists and engineers use for the battery looks like the voltaic pile. To students who have built the pile, this symbol will be especially meaningful.

PREPARATION

Before class, if necessary, cut the zinc plates so that they are 7.5 x 7.5 centimeters and the copper plates so that they are 10 x 10 centimeters. (The copper plates are larger than the zinc plates in order to prevent any spilled liquid from contacting the copper.) —→ *? Running off the copper.?*

Make saturated salt water by mixing one cup of water with ¼ cup of salt. Then, for each small group of students, prepare ½ cup of vinegar.

Lay the aluminum foil on a table in a central part of the room. Make sure that the four water-filled soda bottles are completely dry and then place them on the foil to hold up the voltaic pile. Keep the cup of salt water nearby.

LAUNCHING THE LESSON

Tell students the story of Volta, which you will find in the *History* section. Then announce that the class will build its own voltaic pile, one that will shock just like the first pile Volta made. Explain that a good voltaic pile must have at least 20 cells. Have each group of students make one cell to contribute to the pile.

STUDENT ACTIVITY

Divide the zinc, copper, and towels among the students. Place the containers of vinegar around the room, each accessible to four or five students. Then give these directions for creating a cell:

1. Fold a paper-towel section so that it is slightly smaller than the copper *zinc* plate. (Folded, it should be about 8 layers thick.) *Total height 20 x .25 = 5"*

2. Submerge the paper towel in vinegar and squeeze out the excess by pressing down the towel. The towel should be moist but not dripping wet, or it will leak when it is compressed in the pile.

3. With one hand, place the wet towel in the center of a copper plate. With your other hand, which should be kept dry, place the zinc on top of the towel. You have now made one cell. Be sure the cell is perfectly dry on the top of the zinc and the bottom of the copper.

paper towel soaked in vinegar — zinc — copper

Now, give these directions for creating the voltaic pile:

4. Take turns stacking each voltaic cell, zinc side up, on the aluminum foil. As the pile grows, surround it with the soda bottles to keep it from falling.

5. When 20 cells have been stacked, place a paperweight on top of the pile.

Note: wipe excess vinegar from edges of copper plates (check bottom plates!), to prevent vinegar from wicking between copper & zinc plate!!

As students watch, connect one test lead from the aluminum underneath the pile to the topmost zinc piece. This helps get the pile going. Just before the first student tries the shock, disconnect the test lead from the top copper plate but keep it connected to the aluminum underneath.

This is a good time to pause and introduce some terminology. Tell students that their cells, now stacked 20 high, make a voltaic pile—otherwise known as a battery. A battery is simply 2 or more cells connected together. Because the cells are connected zinc-to-copper, we say they are connected in series.

Before giving students directions for feeling the shock, review the following safety procedures:

SAFETY PROCEDURES
- Keep one hand behind your back or in a pocket at all times when charging or discharging the capacitor.
- Always wear rubber-soled shoes.
- Never charge or discharge the capacitor if you are wet or perspiring.
- Feel the shock with one hand only. Do **not** discharge the capacitor with two hands.

Invite students to come up one at a time to experience the pile's shock. Give these directions:

6. Dip the fingers of one hand into the salt water. Put the other hand in your pocket or behind your back.

7. Hold the alligator clip in the palm of your hand with three fingers. This part of your hand should be connected to the bottom terminal of the pile by means of the wire (terminal simply means the end.) Extend your index finger, and touch it to the top terminal—the uppermost zinc plate. Feel the shock.

8. Feel how increasing the number of cells between the wire and your finger increases the shock: Still holding the alligator clip in the palm of your hand, start at the bottom of the pile and run your index finger up the side of the voltaic pile.

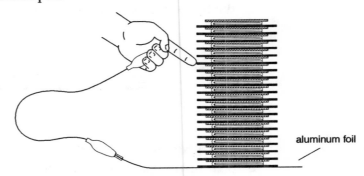

aluminum foil

The shock will increase. You will probably feel a small tingle at about 10 cells and a small shock at 20 cells. Tell students that each cell contributes approximately one volt of shocking force; the word *volt* makes sense because one volt comes from one voltaic cell. At this point students should realize that the more cells between the bottom of the pile and the finger that is touching the pile, the more volts there are, and the stronger the shock will be.

When students have completed the activity, have them dismantle the pile. The metals must be thoroughly rinsed and allowed to air dry, and the towels should be thrown away. (If a voltaic pile sits for any length of time, a good deal of bothersome corrosion will accumulate on the plates.)

Troubleshooting

Here are some problems that students may encounter:

• *The voltaic pile won't shock.* This may occur because the pile is "shorted out" by leakage. If so, identify those cells that are dripping vinegar and remove them. The problem may be that the pile contains one or more cells that are too dry. Take apart the pile and examine each cell. Put more vinegar on towels that seem too dry. Since the problem may be caused by some cells that are upside down, check to make sure every cell is right side up.

• *Some students feel the shock while others don't.* A student may not have dipped his or her fingers in the salt water. Thumb and index finger should be rubbed together in the salt water, which should then be worked into the skin before student tries again. If, due to excitement, a student has jammed a finger on the pile, the student should touch the pile again slowly and lightly.

MAKING CONNECTIONS

Ask questions such as these to help students retain the information they will need for subsequent lessons:

• *What did you feel when you touched the top and bottom of the voltaic pile?*

• *What is the relationship between the number of cells between your fingers and how hard the voltaic pile shocks?*

• *When the cells are piled up one on top of the other, zinc-to-copper, zinc-to-copper, are they connected in series or in parallel?*

• *If each cell contributes approximately one volt to the pile, approximately how many volts of shock does the whole pile produce?*

• *What is the relationship between the number of volts and the shock?*

• *Do you think the voltaic-pile effect is electric in nature? Explain your thinking.*

FOR FURTHER INVESTIGATION

Supervise students closely as they try the following activity:

• Build a shocking voltaic pile using 30 cells of aluminum foil and nickels instead of zinc and copper plates. Cut paper-towel segments the size of pennies and dip them in vinegar. Stack the cells into a voltaic pile and follow the same procedure as described in the *Student Activity* section.

HISTORY

In 1791, in Bologna, Italy, a professor of anatomy named Luigi Galvani made a startling and serendipitous discovery. He inserted a brass hook into a pair of frog's legs and then hung the frog's legs by the hook on an iron fence. He noticed that the legs jumped at precisely the moment they touched the fence! Galvani knew of only one thing that could make the frog's legs jump—an electric charge. But where did the charge come from? He concluded that it must have been stored in the frog's legs and that, somehow, touching the metals allowed this "animal electricity" to leak out.

Galvani published his findings. He went so far as to claim that the electricity in the frog's legs was some sort of life force. The scientific community was astounded, and Galvani's fame spread rapidly. Alessandro Volta, a physicist from a nearby city, was particularly intrigued. Volta agreed with Galvani that electricity had made the frog's legs jump, but Volta was unconvinced by Galvani's explanation.

Volta set out to prove that the electricity was produced by the two metals that touched Galvani's frog's legs. In a series of ingenious experiments, Volta showed that two different metals could acquire opposite electric charges when touched together and pulled apart. However, these charges were very slight and could be detected only by a very sensitive electroscope. Although Volta had convinced himself that the metals produced an electric charge, he knew it would be hard to convince others. Why? Mostly because, at the time, electricity was the stuff of Leyden jars and spinning static-charge machines. In other words, electricity was the stuff that shocked! So how was Volta to show the scientific world that his new battery produced electricity?

Volta's answer was to find a way to make the metals shock. After a great deal of experimentation, he found that he could pile pairs of metals, such as zinc and copper, on top of each other. He separated the metals in each pair by a towel soaked in acid. If enough pairs of metals were piled, they would deliver a convincing shock. This pile of metal pairs was named the voltaic pile, which we now call a battery.

When Volta made his findings public, scientists throughout the world duplicated his discovery and were truly amazed. The voltaic pile seemed like a capacitor that never needed charging! Even more startling, the pile produced a continuous flow of charge.

In short order, Volta's discovery quickly eclipsed Galvani's. Galvani's theory of animal electricity came to be widely disregarded, and Galvani himself died relatively poor and disgraced. Still, Galvani deserved immense credit for making the first observation of "current electricity."

·14· *Big Cell, No Shock*

Cells in Parallel

Time **Thirty minutes**

MATERIALS
For the entire class:

20 zinc and 20 copper plates (or 10-20 AA-cells and 1 roll of masking tape)

20 paper towels

1 quart of white vinegar

1 cup of water

¼ cup of salt

5-6 cups

2 sheets of aluminum foil, each approximately 3 ½′ x 1′

2 test leads

OVERVIEW
Students will reconstruct 20 voltaic cells and connect them in parallel. They will discover that cells in parallel don't shock because the voltage is not increased. They will then refine their definition of voltage as the push on an electron.

TEACHER BACKGROUND
Twenty voltaic cells, piled in series, produce a perceivable shock. Yet the same 20 cells connected in parallel and placed side by side, as shown on page 64, won't shock at all. It is this phenomenon that prompts us to look more closely at the concept of voltage. The question to be answered is this: Why won't 20 cells, connected in parallel, shock?

In order to answer this question, it is necessary to understand that the number of volts describes the force with which the electrons push through a circuit. By connecting the cells in series, that is, by stacking them on top of each other, we can increase the voltage they supply. However, if the cells are connected in parallel, they form, in essence, one big cell. Despite its large size, this one big cell supplies only one volt of push, just as a small cell does. And one volt is not enough push for an appreciable electron flow.

In this lesson, you are giving students an opportunity to intuit the concept of voltage. This is difficult, but it is not impossible if you guide students' thinking when they come together during the *Making Connections* section. Almost assuredly your students have seen the word *volt* before on warning signs, on appliances, and so forth. It is easy to assume that voltage is the amount of electricity, or the size of the electron flow. Students should come to realize that voltage is not the quantity of electricity but the force with which electrons are being pushed, usually through a circuit. It has been the author's experience, time and again, that when students attempt to reason why a pile of 20 cells in series shocks but 20 cells in parallel do not, the idea that the pile pushes the charge harder occurs naturally. This idea of push is the seed for understanding voltage.

By having the opportunity to intuit the concept of voltage themselves, without the modern advantages of multimeters or even light bulbs, students may well come away with a profound and long-lasting understanding.

PREPARATION

Follow the steps in the *Preparation* section of Lesson 13, *A New Shock*. This time, the sheet of aluminum foil will require more table space.

LAUNCHING THE LESSON

Ask students to recall the number of cells in the voltaic pile and the differences in the resulting shocks when touching the cells lower down or near the top of the pile. Have students predict what kind of shock would result if the cells were laid out flat in two rows of 10. Students should give reasons for their thinking.

STUDENT ACTIVITY

Distribute the zinc and copper plates, paper towels, and vinegar so that students can make the voltaic cells. Invite students to bring their cells to the work table. But instead of having them construct a pile, or a series of cells, direct students to connect the 20 cells together in parallel as follows:

1. Lay out the 20 cells on top of one piece of aluminum foil. Each cell should be laid copper-side down so that the aluminum foil connects all 20 copper plates together. The bottom layer will actually be like one big copper piece.

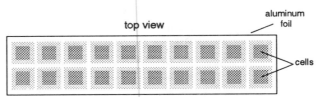

2. Place the second piece of aluminum foil over the tops of the cells without touching the paper towels or copper at any point. When you are done, you will have made one big cell with one huge bottom layer of copper and one huge top layer of zinc. In other words, you will have connected the cells in parallel.

3. What do you expect to happen when different students wet their fingers with salt water and touch the top and bottom layers of the battery? Try it and see. (There is no shock.)

4. Clean up as soon as possible. Carefully wash and dry the zinc and copper plates.

MAKING CONNECTIONS

This discussion needs to be heavily teacher directed. By the end of the lesson, students should realize that voltage is essentially the push on an electron. They should also understand that the parallel battery does not shock because, although huge, it is really one big cell with the voltage of one cell. The voltaic pile, on the other hand, is a battery of cells in series, and it shocks because the series connection raises the voltage.

To develop students' understanding, do the following:

On the chalkboard, sketch a side view of the parallel battery shown on page 64. Explain that the 20 cells are connected in parallel. Since all of the copper plates are connected together, effectively making one large copper piece, and all of the zinc plates are connected together, effectively making one large zinc piece, the 20 cells are essentially one big cell.

Ask:

• *Why doesn't the battery of cells in parallel shock? Why did the same cells shock when they were stacked in a pile?* (Students will suggest that somehow the battery of cells in series—the voltaic pile—has greater voltage than the battery of cells in parallel. If necessary, tell students that one cell produces about one volt, and the cells in parallel are essentially one big cell.)

• *How many volts would one cell the size of a tennis court produce?* (The answer is that it can only produce one volt.)

• *If higher voltage means greater shock, what is voltage?* (A typical response would be that voltage is the quantity of electricity. If students believe this, point out that the parallel batteries contained the same amount of zinc and copper to produce the electron flow, indicating that voltage is not the quantity of the electron flow.)

• *If voltage is not the size of the current, then what is voltage?* (Guide students to an understanding that voltage is the push of electrons through the circuit. A single cell, with one volt, simply doesn't push electrons hard enough to go through skin and produce a shock. A 20-cell series battery—the voltaic pile producing 20 volts—does.)

Now recap the discussion by having volunteers write the following points on the chalkboard:

• Connecting cells in series increases the overall voltage, as in the voltaic pile.

• Cells connected in parallel have the same overall voltage as one cell.

• Voltage is the push on an electron, not the size of an electron flow.

Inside a Flashlight "Battery"

How a Dry Cell Works

Time **Thirty minutes**

MATERIALS

For the teacher demonstration:

1 used, nonalkaline D-cell—commonly called a flashlight battery—(or any cells labeled "Heavy Duty" or "Long Life," sizes C, A, AA, AAA; do not use alkaline batteries)

1 9-volt, nonalkaline rectangular battery

1 needlenose pliers (or any kind of pliers)

newspaper (or any disposable table cover)

safety goggles

1 pair of rubber gloves

OVERVIEW

As you take apart a common flashlight cell, students will carefully observe and conclude that its structure is similar to that of the voltaic cell. Based on what they have seen, students will explain how batteries of greater voltages are commonly made.

TEACHER BACKGROUND

A battery is defined as two or more cells connected together. So, technically, the ubiquitous cylindrical 1.5-volt flashlight "battery" is, of course, not a battery at all. It is actually a cell, surprisingly similar in structure to the voltaic cell. The common, smaller, rectangular 9-volt battery, on the other hand, is a real battery comprised of a pile of six cells stacked one on top of another.

CAUTION

For safety reasons, this lesson is designed to be a demonstration only. Wear rubber gloves when performing the dissection. Do not dismantle an alkaline cell such as a Duracell battery.

PREPARATION

Lay out newspaper, rubber gloves, safety goggles, and pliers for the battery dissection.

LAUNCHING THE LESSON

Hold up the D-cell and the 9-volt rectangular battery for the class to see. Point out that the D-cell is labeled 1.5 volts, yet the much smaller

9-volt battery is labeled 9 volts. Invariably, students wonder how the smaller battery can have a greater voltage. Tell students that they are about to find out. First, you will dismantle the D-cell and see what is inside; then you will take apart the 9-volt battery.

TEACHER DEMONSTRATION

Ask students to observe closely as you, wearing goggles and gloves, demonstrate the dismantling of the D-cell:

1. Using pliers, peel the steel top and the cardboard, plastic, or steel casing from the sides, revealing the zinc can and a plastic top.

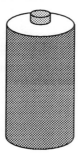

2. Pull off the plastic top and remove the carbon rod. (If no carbon rod is apparent at this point, stop. You may have dismantled an alkaline cell!)

3. Use a pencil to scrape the black paste away from the zinc can, and remove the paper separator. Depending on the brand of D-cell, you may find gel instead of paper between the black paste and the zinc can. Lay all of the components out on the newspaper.

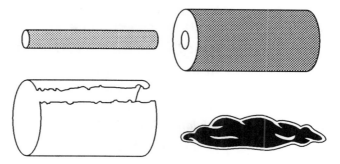

4. Copy the following drawing on the chalkboard to compare the D-cell to the voltaic cell:

Explain that the black paste is actually a mixture containing a metallic compound called manganese dioxide. If students mentally unfold the D-cell, they can see that it is very similar to the copper-and-zinc voltaic cell they made previously. Point out that it is the combination of zinc and manganese metals in the D-cell that gives it the characteristic 1.5 volts. (Every different combination of metals has its own characteristic voltage.)

5. List the components of the D-cell on the chalkboard and then ask students to suggest the analogous parts in the voltaic cell. (D-cell components: zinc can, black paste—typically a mix of ammonium chloride, metal compound (manganese dioxide), water, and carbon separator paper or gel; voltaic cell components: zinc plate, copper plate, paper towel, vinegar)

6. Hold up the 9-volt battery and ask someone to explain, or guess, how this small battery can provide 9 volts, whereas the bigger D-cell only provides 1.5 volts. If no one has a suggestion, here are two clues to offer students: Both the D-cell and the 9-volt battery are made of zinc and manganese. The 9-volt is rightfully called a battery.

7. Continue the demonstration by removing the metal skin and top of a 9-volt battery. Slide the inner package out. One battery contains 6 cells in series, each 1.5 volts (6 cells x 1.5 volts per cell = 9 volts). Both alkaline and nonalkaline cells use one of two possible constructions: either a pile or cylindrical cells in series.

The 6 cells of a 9-volt battery

MAKING CONNECTIONS

To make sure students understand the demonstration, ask questions such as these:

• *How can 6 cells, each supplying 1.5 volts, be used to make a 9-volt battery?* (If the cells are connected in series, the voltage is multiplied: 1.5 x 6 = 9.)

• *What does it mean to say that the small 9-volt battery is a voltaic pile in a can?*

• *How would you construct a 3-volt battery from 1.5-volt cells?* (Connect two 1.5-volt cells in series.) *What about a 12-volt or a 15-volt battery?*

• *How can the small, rectangular, 9-volt battery deliver more voltage than the much larger 1.5-volt D-cell?*

• *Why do you think it is acceptable to call the 9-volt battery a battery, yet unacceptable to call the 1.5-volt cell a battery?* (Only the 9-volt battery is made up of more than a single cell.)

FOR FURTHER INVESTIGATION

Obtain a dead 6-volt lantern battery and do another demonstration. Have students predict what they will find out about its construction when you dismantle it. Remove the battery's metal skin with pliers. You will see four cells, each like a large D-cell. Have students trace the connections from cell to cell. Students should find that the four cells are connected in series.

·16·

Chlorine from a Drop

Investigating the Voltaic Pile

Time **One period**

MATERIALS

For each small group of students:

1 6-volt lantern battery (or 4 1.5-volt cells connected in series or any low-voltage dc power supply)

2 test leads (or 2 homemade aluminum foil wires)

1 drop of salt water*

1 overhead transparency (or 1 plastic bag or any nonconducting plastic)*

2 pencil-point electrodes

For teacher also*

OVERVIEW

Students will use one kind of voltaic pile—a lantern battery—to determine that the flow of electricity from a battery is continuous and to understand that this flow is called the current. Students demonstrate that current can cause chemical reactions.

TEACHER BACKGROUND

To electrolyze a solution of salt water is literally to break the molecules with electricity. In a practical sense, this means that students use a battery to make trace amounts of chlorine and hydrogen gases from a drop of salt water. Students can easily detect the chlorine gas by its characteristic swimming-pool odor.

Electrolysis, or electricity-breaking, can help students learn more about the nature of the voltaic battery and the electron flow it produces. By observing the bubble formation in a water drop, it becomes readily apparent that the flow of charge through the wires is continuous.

PREPARATION

Cut a large overhead transparency into 3-inch x 3-inch pieces, one for each group of students. Prepare a cup of salt water.

LAUNCHING THE LESSON

Explain to students that the voltaic pile very quickly led to a number of discoveries. Ask students to imagine that they are scientists in the year 1800 and that they have been given one of the world's first voltaic piles—in this case, a 6-volt lantern battery. Tell students that they will also have test leads, small pieces of graphite from a pencil, and salt water. Their task will be to make discoveries.

STUDENT ACTIVITY

Distribute the materials to each group. Then give the following directions:

1. Break off a piece of wood and graphite below the wood line on the pencil. Strip away the wood, leaving only the graphite. Insert the graphite into one end of a test lead. Do the same for the other pencil. These are pencil-point electrodes.

2. Attach the other ends of the test leads to the lantern battery.

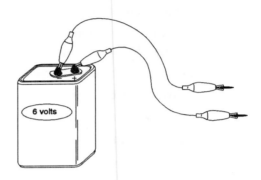

As students do this, go around the room and place a drop of salt water about the size of a quarter on each group's transparency.

3. You now have two electrodes attached to the battery and one salt water drop. Using just these materials, see what you can discover. Make sure the steel part of the alligator clips doesn't touch the salt water because they can easily corrode.

Allow students to experiment for about 15 minutes as you circulate among them. It is likely that students will discover the following:

• They can make bubbles. (Students will have inserted the pencil-point electrodes into the water drop. If the electrodes do not touch each other, students will see bubbles forming at each electrode.)

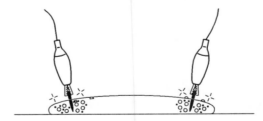

• The bubbles stop. (By touching the electrodes inside the water drop, students will observe that the bubbles stop forming.)
• The bubbles have a strong smell. (Students may identify the odor with that of a swimming pool or may name it chlorine gas.)
• The bubbles with the chlorine smell come from the test lead attached to

the positive terminal of the battery. (When students insert the electrodes as far apart as possible, they can smell that the chlorine comes from the positive terminal only—the one connected to the copper. The gas at the other electrode is hydrogen.)

MAKING CONNECTIONS

Bring the groups together to discuss the discoveries they made. Help students learn from these discoveries by asking questions such as these:

• *What can you learn by seeing that the bubbles can flow continuously in the water drop?* (This is evidence that there is a continuous flow of electricity from the battery. Tell students that the flow of electricity from the battery is called the current. More precisely, it is an electron flow.)

• *What can you learn by seeing that current flowing through salt water produces gases?* (This suggests that electricity can cause a chemical reaction.)

• *Why did the bubbles stop when the two pencil-point electrodes touched each other?* (The charge passes directly from one electrode to the other. When the electrodes don't touch, the charge must pass through the solution. At this point, you can reinforce students' understanding of the term *electrode*. In this case, the electrodes are the pencil points that were inserted into the water.)

• *Why does the chlorine gas always come from the liquid near the electrode that is attached to the copper terminal?* (This indicates that the copper always assumes a certain charge—positive or negative—and that this charge is necessary for the production of chlorine gas.)

• *What could be the source of the chlorine smell?* (You most likely will have to tell students that salt [NaCl] is made of sodium [Na] and chlorine [Cl]. In effect, the salt in the water drop is split by the electron flow. The sodium stays in the solution, and the chlorine escapes as a gas.)

FOR FURTHER INVESTIGATION

Have each group do the experiment again in one of the four following ways:

• Exchange the pencil-point electrodes for steel paper clips. Put these paper-clip electrodes into a very small drop of salt water.

• Use pennies as electrodes in place of the pencil points.

• Use pencil-point electrodes. Change the content of the water. Mix a teaspoon of washing soda, not baking soda, into a quarter cup of water. What happens this time when the pencil-point electrodes are placed into a spot of this water?

• Repeat the experiment, but use plain tap water. (When paper clips are used, the water turns a green-brown because iron atoms from the paper clips enter into the reaction. When pennies are used, the water turns yellow because copper enters from the pennies. When pencil-point electrodes are used, vigorous bubbling occurs at the sites of both electrodes, and the gases produced are hydrogen and oxygen. With plain tap water, relatively few bubbles are produced.)

HISTORY

Literally just days after Volta's pile was introduced to the scientific community, experimenters made another remarkable discovery: When a wire was connected to the bottom of the pile and its other end was put into a drop of water on the top of the pile, wildly active bubbles formed. After investigating further, scientists collected a gas that could explode with a pop—a sure sign of the presence of hydrogen.

This phenomenon was named electrolysis, meaning "electric breaking." Although at the time the exact chemical mechanisms were not fully understood, electrolysis was soon used to isolate a number of reactive elements for the first time—a major advancement in the understanding of chemistry.

What is Voltaic Electricity?

Conductors and Insulators Revisited

Time **One period**

MATERIALS

For each small group of students:

1 6-volt lantern battery (or 1 9-volt transistor batter or 4 D-cells in series)

3 test leads (or 3 homemade aluminum foil wires)

1 drop of salt water*

2 pencil-point electrodes (or 2 mechanical pencil leads or paper clips)

1 overhead transparency (or 1 plastic bag or other nonconducting plastic)*

various conductors and insulators identified in Unit 1, Lesson 11*

For teacher also*

OVERVIEW

Students will compile evidence showing that static and current electricity are essentially the same and that the conductivity of substances depends on the voltage applied.

Whereas students previously classified conductors and insulators with the Leyden jar, they will now use the same objects to test their batteries. Will an object that insulates electricity produced by the capacitor also prevent this new kind of electricity from flowing? Will a capacitor conductor conduct voltaic electricity? The answers to these questions will help students determine how closely related these two kinds of electricity really are.

TEACHER BACKGROUND

The big difference between currents produced by the homemade capacitor and the lantern battery is voltage. If you were to measure the voltage of a fully charged, homemade capacitor on a static voltmeter, you would discover that it charges to between 5,000 and 10,000 volts. Compare this to the lantern battery, which supplies a mere 6 volts.

Substances identified as insulators with the capacitor also insulate at only 6 volts. However, some substances that conduct at 10,000 volts will not conduct at 6 volts. This can serve to further demonstrate that voltage is the push on electrons in a circuit.

PREPARATION

As in Lesson 4, prepare 3" x 3" overhead transparencies and a cup of salt water. Locate and display the lists of conductors and insulators from

Lesson 11 in Unit 1. Gather the same materials used for that lesson.

LAUNCHING THE LESSON

Draw students' attention to the list of conductors and insulators that they compiled in Unit 1. Ask students to predict what they would find if they were to use a 6-volt battery to retest these items. Would insulators still behave as insulators? Would conductors of electricity from a capacitor also conduct voltaic electricity? Does the electricity of the battery act like the electricity of the capacitor?

STUDENT ACTIVITY

Distribute materials to each group of students and then give the following directions:

1. Gather objects from the list of conductors and insulators used with the capacitor. Choose those you would like to test with a lantern battery.

2. Construct the electrolysis circuit from a battery and pencil-point electrodes as you did in the *Student Activity* section of Lesson 16.

3. Put a drop of water on each group's transparency.

4. Select an object to test for conductivity and insert it into the circuit. Carefully observe the electrodes in the drop of water. Do bubbles form? Does this make your object a conductor or an insulator?

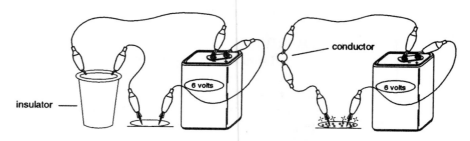

5. Try other objects and record whether they are insulators or conductors.

MAKING CONNECTIONS

Choose from among the following questions as you guide a discussion of the activity:

• *What evidence do you have that the voltaic pile has the same kind of electricity as the capacitor?* (The voltaic pile and the capacitor share many conductors and insulators. Both the capacitor and the voltaic pile shock.)

• *How is the voltaic pile different from the capacitor?* (The feeling of the shock is different. The voltaic pile is self-charging. Not all conductors identified with the capacitor conduct the voltaic pile's electricity.)

• *Are there objects that insulated the capacitor's current but conducted the battery's current?* (Probably not.)

• *Which, if any, objects conducted the capacitor's current but insulated the battery's current?* (It is quite likely that students found some objects that did just this.)

• *It can be demonstrated with an appropriate measuring instrument that the capacitor is charged to between 5,000 and 10,000 volts. How can this fact be used to explain why some objects conduct with the capacitor but insulate with the battery?* (Voltage is the push on the electrons in the circuit. At 10,000 volts, electrons are pushing hard enough to get through a certain substance; but at only 6 volts, the electrons may not be pushing hard enough to get through. Conductivity is not absolute but depends upon the voltage applied.)

• *How do you think current electricity is different from static electricity? How are the two similar?* (An electric current is a continuous flow of charges, usually through a wire, whereas static electricity involves charges that don't flow continuously. Although static charges are usually stationary, they can move. When they do, the resulting current is usually a momentary one.)

FOR FURTHER INVESTIGATION

Some groups may want to retest substances that were probably identified as poor conductors with the capacitor—for example, motor oil and vaseline. Often, these substances will not conduct in a circuit with the voltaic pile. The reason, which will later become clear, is that the capacitor has much higher voltage than the voltaic pile, meaning that the electrons are pushing harder to get through.

HISTORY

Does the voltaic pile produce a new and different kind of electricity from that of the capacitor? No. We now know that both the capacitor and the voltaic pile produce a flow of electrons. But early nineteenth-century scientists spoke of "voltaic electricity," otherwise known as "galvanic electricity," as something apart from the "regular" electricity collected and released by a capacitor.

·18· Current Mysteries

The Origin of Current

Time **One period**

MATERIALS

For each small group of students:

1 6-volt lantern battery (or 4 1.5-volt cells connected in series or any low voltage dc power supply)*

1 test lead (or 1 homemade foil wire)*

1 cup of white vinegar (or 1 cup of water containing 1 tsp salt)*

3-4 zinc plates 7.5 cm square

3-4 copper-plates 10 cm square

3-4 paper towels

For the whole class:
books on electricity or physics containing text and pictures that reveal the difference between current and electron flow

For teacher also*

OVERVIEW

The purpose of this lesson is to answer two main questions: How does a battery produce a current? What is current and how is it different from electron flow? Students will reconstruct voltaic cells and examine them for evidence of chemical reaction.

TEACHER BACKGROUND

The difference between current and electron flow often confuses students, and for good reason. Current describes the rate at which electric charges flow past a certain point. By convention, the direction of an electric current is defined as the direction in which the positive charges flow: Current is said to flow out of the positive terminal of a battery, through the circuit, and into the negative terminal. However, as we know, the negative charges—the electrons—do the flowing. Electrons flow out of the negative terminal of a battery and into the positive terminal, in the opposite direction of the current. But ever since Benjamin Franklin designated electrons as positive, the current has been defined as the flow of positive charge. This terminology has simply continued to this day.

There is another question worth clearing up before going on: How does a battery produce a current? If students look carefully for clues, they can see evidence of a chemical reaction having taken place on the zinc and copper pieces. It is, in fact, a chemical reaction that produces the current. When students have mastered the various terms and ideas in this lesson, they will be better prepared to communicate with other people who study electricity.

PREPARATION

Gather dictionaries, encyclopedias, and books on electricity as described in the *Materials* section. Write the following questions on the chalkboard:

• *What is a current and how is it different from an electron flow?*

• *How does a battery produce a current?*

You may want each group to conduct the research and discuss it among themselves during one entire period. Then, during the next period, after students complete the activity, they can use this information to enrich the discussion.

Have the 6-volt battery and the test lead ready for the discussion in the *Making Connections* section.

LAUNCHING THE LESSON

After students have had a chance to offer comments and speculate about the answers to the questions on the chalkboard, have them research the questions and discuss their findings with their group members.

STUDENT ACTIVITY

Tell students to work with the same groups as before while they continue with the activity. Challenge students to keep the questions on the chalkboard in mind as you present the following directions:

1. With your group, construct as many voltaic cells as your material allows, just as you did for the voltaic pile. Then stack all your group's cells in a pile, connect a test lead from one terminal to the other, and allow it to run for about 20 minutes. If you listen carefully, you may be able to hear a fizzing sound coming from the cells.

2. At the end of this time, take the cells apart and examine them carefully. Talk over and record what you find.

MAKING CONNECTIONS

Encourage students to draw together what they have learned both through research and investigation. Discuss answers to the two questions on the chalkboard.

At this point, students will probably be able to answer some or all of the following questions:

• *How did the copper and zinc plates look different before and after you ran the voltaic pile?* (Before making the cells, the zinc and copper plates were relatively clear. Afterwards, there were green-blue deposits on the copper and white-gray deposits on the zinc. Zinc reacts chemically with the vinegar and gains extra electrons. A reaction between the copper and the vinegar takes electrons from the copper. Thus, the zinc becomes negatively charged with extra electrons, and the copper becomes positively charged, requiring electrons.)

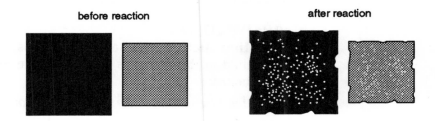

before reaction   after reaction

• *When the zinc and copper are connected with a wire, electrons flow out of the zinc, through the wire, and into the copper. Why does this occur?* (Like charges repel. The extra electrons in the zinc repel one another, so they will spread out into the wire. Opposite charges attract. The positively charged copper plate attracts the electrons from the zinc plate, pulling them through the wire.)

• *Why do the electrons keep flowing in the voltaic pile?* (What is most peculiar about the voltaic cell is that the electron flow is continuous. As the zinc is relieved of its extra electrons, the chemical reaction starts again and replaces those electrons carried away. So the supply of extra electrons in the zinc is continuously renewed. Likewise, the positive charge on the copper is constantly renewed. As electrons stream in, they are consumed by the further reaction between vinegar and copper, causing the copper to keep its positive charge. Eventually, all of the reactants will be consumed. When this happens, the cell will no longer be able to produce a current.)

• *What is current? How is it different from electron flow?* (Current is the rate at which charges flow past a certain point, or the rate of the electron flow. Many people use the word *current* interchangeably with *electron flow*. Although these terms are virtually the same, there is one important difference. By convention, current is said to be the flow of charge from positive to negative. This is simply a matter of terminology. In truth, of course, it is the flow of charge from negative to positive.)

You might want to have students look again at the questions on the chalkboard and express any problems in understanding the concepts developed in the lesson. Other students may then be able to suggest solutions.

·19· A Hot Time

Investigating Resistance

Time Two periods

MATERIALS
For each small group of students:

1 6-volt lantern battery (or 4 D-cells connected in series)*

10 mechanical pencil leads*

6 test leads (or 6 homemade foil wires)*

1 pair of scissors

For each student:

1 thick drinking straw (or 1 rolled piece of paper)

1 thin drinking straw (or 1 hollow coffee stirrer)

For teacher also*

OVERVIEW
Students will discover that current flowing through a resistor produces heat and that a resistor reduces the size of the current through all points in the circuit. Students will go on to determine both the effect on the current of resistors in series and in parallel. They will also investigate how a resistor's length and thickness affect its resistance.

TEACHER BACKGROUND
What causes an electric stove or a hair dryer to heat up? The answer has to do with resistance. Any substance through which electrons flow—for example, a copper wire, a paper clip, or a carbon rod—tends to hold back, or resist, the electron flow. When electrons do push through a resistor, they produce heat by exciting the atoms of the resistor as they pass through, creating, in essence, electric friction.

By doing a number of experiments with mechanical pencil leads and batteries, students can determine that resistors in series resist more than a single resistor. They can also discover that two resistors in parallel resist less than a single resistor.

In this activity, an effort has been made to create experiments similar to those that scientists in the early 1800s might have carried out. In those days, there were no electronic multimeters to measure current or resistance; scientists had only their senses and their intuition. It might be tempting to let students simply watch a meter's needle rise or fall. However, allowing them to feel, see, and even smell evidence of resistance may well make a longer and deeper impression.

PREPARATION

Set up the first step in the *Student Activity* section without completing the circuit so that students can duplicate it.

LAUNCHING THE LESSON

Ask students to recall what they observe inside a toaster when it toasts bread. Ask students what is so special about the little wires inside the toaster. Why do they get so hot while the outside wire stays cool? Explain that by experimenting with pencil lead, students will be able to answer these questions.

Call students' attention to the circuit you have set up and especially to the pencil lead. Tell them the lead is called a resistor because it offers resistance. Then ask students to consider what will happen if they run an electric current through the resistor. After they make predictions or guesses, tell them to experiment to find out.

STUDENT ACTIVITY

Distribute materials to each group of students and then give the following directions:

1. Set up the battery and alligator clips as you see me doing and then complete the circuit.

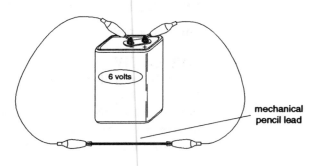

mechanical
pencil lead

> **CAUTION**
> Warn students not to touch the lead or the bottom part of the alligator clips that hold the lead. These both get very hot.

You may want to demonstrate to students that the lead is so hot that it can burn a line through a small piece of paper.

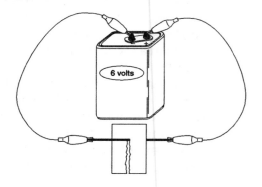

2. Discuss with other group members what happened to the lead when a current flowed through your circuit. Try to explain why the resistor gets so hot.

3. Predict what would happen to the circuit if you put resistors in series—meaning one after the other—so that the current has to flow through each in turn. Then set up this circuit and find out what happens.

Disconnect this circuit and allow it to cool down afterwards.

4. Predict what would happen to the circuit if you put 3, 4, or 5 resistors in the circuit—again, all in series. Then set these up one at a time and see what happens.

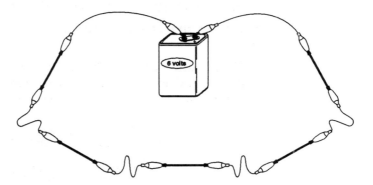

Disconnect the circuit and let it cool down between each experiment.

5. Which resists more, a long resistor or a short resistor? To find out, first set up the circuit with 5 resistors, hooking them up at the ends so that the current runs the entire length of each resistor. Proceeding carefully, feel the heat. Then disconnect and let the resistors cool down. Next, move the alligator clips together on each pencil-lead resistor so that the alligator clips are about 1 inch apart. (This shortens each resistor.) Again, carefully feel the heat. How does it compare to the heat when the resistors are longer?

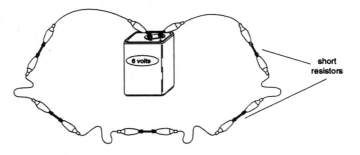

short resistors

6. Will 2 identical resistors in parallel resist less or more than a single resistor? Find out by building another circuit with 5 resistors. Add another pencil lead to each resistor so that you have a series of 5 resistors in parallel. Each resistor will now have 2 leads side by side. Close the circuit and feel the heat.

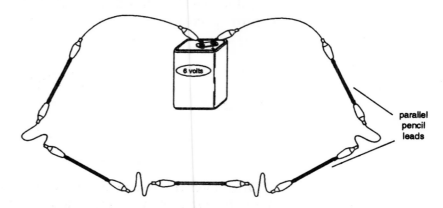

parallel
pencil
leads

7. Pick up your 2 straws. Blow first through the thin straw first and then the thick one. Imagine the air is an electric current, or the flow of electrons. Which straw is harder to blow through?

8. Cut the thin straw 1 inch shorter. Is it easier or harder to blow through now?

9. Keep cutting an inch off the thin straw and then blowing through it. Is a shorter resistor easier to blow through than a longer resistor? Draw the following 4 resistors on the chalkboard:

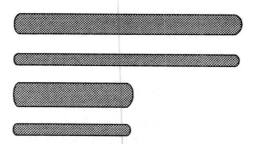

10. Imagine that these are resistors, all carbon rods. Which carbon rod will resist the most? Which would resist the least? (Students will probably agree that the long and thin rod resists the most and the short thick rod, the least.)

MAKING CONNECTIONS

Ask students to recall what happened in their experiments as they answer the following questions:

• *In a circuit containing one resistor, what happens to the resistor when the current flows?* (It gets hot.)

• *What happens when you add more resistors in series?* (The more resistors there are, the less heat is produced. All the resistors have the same amount of heat.)

• *How does the length of a resistor affect the heat production?* (The shorter resistor heats up more quickly, resists less, and produces less heat.)

• *How does adding resistors in parallel affect the current flow?* (Resistors in parallel resist less and allow more current to flow through.)

• *What do your experiments with thick and thin drinking straws help you to understand about how a toaster works?* (After students comment, add that the toaster has a heating element made of thin wires of a metal alloy that resists an electric current; when current flows through these wires, heat is produced.)

• *Why doesn't the power cord get hot?* (It doesn't offer as much resistance because it is much thicker than the heating element wires, and it is made of copper, which offers little resistance to the current.)

FOR FURTHER INVESTIGATION

• Encourage students to find examples of resistors used in their homes. (Resistor heating elements are found in stoves, hair dryers, toasters, electric blankets, heating pads, electric space heaters, and many more devices. In addition, practically all electronic devices, from televisions to computers to copiers, are equipped with 1 or more resistors to protect the components inside them.)

• Offer students this "brain teaser": Can a copper wire resist as much as a carbon rod of the same thickness? Remember that copper is a good conductor, whereas carbon is a poorer conductor. (Some students may correctly say that if the copper wire is very long, it can resist as much as a short carbon rod of the same thickness because the longer the resistor, the more it resists. Point out that every substance except a "superconductor" resists electric current to some extent. Even aluminum, copper, silver, and gold, some of the best natural conductors, still offer some resistance.)

Blowing a Fuse

A Large Current Melts a Thin Wire

Time **Thirty minutes**

MATERIALS

For each small group of students:

6-volt battery (or 24 D-cells in series)

2 test leads (or 2 homemade foil wires)

2 medium-sized steel paper clips (or 2 metal paper clips of any size)

2 2" pieces of masking tape (or 2 pieces of any tape)

1 quarter of a steel-wool pad*

For each student:

1 pair of safety goggles

For teacher also*

OVERVIEW

Students will demonstrate the melting and burning action of a fuse when too much current flows through it, thus opening a circuit in the fuse. A single strand of steel wire quickly ignites with the current from a 6-volt battery. Students will also discuss fuses as devices for protecting machinery and homes from electrical fires.

TEACHER BACKGROUND

If too much current were to flow through the wires of your house or car, the wires could heat up and start a fire. However, modern homes are protected by circuit breakers, which serve the same purpose as fuses but can be reset with a switch. Fuses are thin strands of wire designed to melt safely inside a glass bulb when the current is too great, thereby opening, or breaking, the circuit. Automobiles, electric devices, and some older houses still contain fuses to protect their circuitry.

PREPARATION

If you use a Brillo or SOS pad, wash all of the soap out of it. Dry it thoroughly and quickly with a hair dryer or some other device to prevent rusting.

LAUNCHING THE LESSON

Begin by telling students a disturbing story involving electricity. It is Saturday morning and your family is trying to finish the chores so that everyone can go the beach. Your brother is baking bread, with the oven on "high." You are running the washing machine and the clothes dryer.

Your father has just loaded the dishwasher and turned it on. Your mother is outside cutting boards with her electric circular saw. Your sister is chopping nuts in the blender. The television was left on in the living room. With so many appliances running at the same time, too much current is now flowing through the wires in your home. Behind the walls and in the attic, entirely unseen, wires turn from cold to warm to burning hot. Slowly but surely, some sticks of wood next to the wires slowly catch fire. As you drive off to the beach, you and your family are totally unaware of what is happening.

Halfway to the beach, you realize you have forgotten the towels, so you return home. Luckily, you smell smoke, call the fire department, and prevent your house from burning to its foundation.

Reassure students that, happily, this near disaster rarely occurs. Houses are protected against this type of electrical fire by fuses or circuit breakers. When too many electrical appliances are turned on at once, and too much current begins to flow through the wires in a home, the fuse, or the circuit breaker, automatically opens the circuit. This stops all current from flowing, thereby preventing a fire from starting.

Tell students that in this activity they will make their own fuses so that they can observe what happens when too much current flows through a thin fuse wire.

STUDENT ACTIVITY

Distribute materials to each group and then give the following directions:

1. To assemble the fuse apparatus and circuit, unfold two paper clips like this:

2. Tape the paper clips to the tabletop, so that they are a half a centimeter apart. Use the hookup wires and battery to set up the circuit.

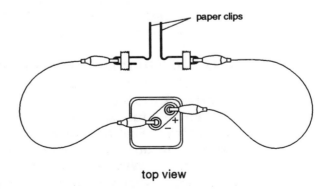

top view

Before students begin to work, explain these safety procedures:

SAFETY PROCEDURES
- Don't use more than one strand of steel wool at a time. Whereas one or two strands will burn harmlessly, many strands together can start a small fire. Iron burns!
- Wear safety glasses at all times, even when you are not actively participating. (Make sure that students wear their safety goggles from this point until the end of the lesson. Remove any student who does not comply with this rule.)
- When burning a steel-wool fuse, keep your face and body as far away from the steel-wool strand as possible. Hold the steel wool with your arms outstretched.
- If you are just observing, watch the fuses burning from a safe distance of at least 3 feet.

When all students indicate their agreement with these safety rules, direct them to burn a fuse as follows:

3. Separate a single strand of steel wool and pull it tightly between the paper clips.

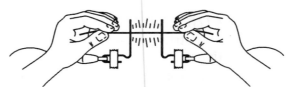

The steel wool should melt with a tiny, fiery display. Be aware that small pieces of sparkling, burning steel may be ejected, some as far as a foot away.

MAKING CONNECTIONS
Have students talk about the experiment and then suggest answers to the following questions:

• *What would happen if the steel-wool strand were 10 times thicker? Would it heat up more quickly or more slowly?*

• *Think about what a fire needs in order to burn. If a large current is flowing through such a thin wire, why doesn't the filament in a flashlight bulb burn out quickly?* (Some students may be able to say that the oxygen has been removed. In order to burn, the wire requires oxygen.)

FOR FURTHER INVESTIGATION
Ask students to conduct the following investigations at home and then report back to the class:
• Examine a fuse box in your home or in an automobile. Why are the fuses there? Find the power cords that lead to a washing machine and dryer. How does the thickness of the wire compare to that of other electrical cords? Why are some cords thicker and some thinner? (Students may suggest that a washer and dryer use so much current that an ordinary thinner power cord would heat up dangerously.)

·21· *The Squeeze-Bottle Model*

How Voltage, Current, and Resistance are Related

Time **Thirty minutes**

MATERIALS
For each student:

1 empty plastic dishwashing detergent bottle with adjustable nozzle (or any plastic squeeze bottle with an adjustable nozzle)*

food coloring*

For teacher also*

OVERVIEW
Students will use squeeze bottles to model Ohm's law, which states the relationship between the voltage, current, and resistance of a circuit.

TEACHER BACKGROUND
What voltage, current, and resistance are, and how they are related, are concepts easily misunderstood. Happily, much of the confusion can be avoided with just an empty dishwashing detergent bottle and some water.

What the squeeze-bottle model demonstrates is usually expressed mathematically as Ohm's law—of central importance to any serious subsequent study of electricity. The formula for Ohm's law can be expressed as $I = E/R$, where I = current, or rate of electron flow, expressed in amperes; E = voltage expressed in volts; and R = resistance expressed in ohms.

PREPARATION
Fill each of the squeeze bottles with colored water. Replace the top.

LAUNCHING THE LESSON
Hold up a squeeze bottle filled with water and ask students whether they believe that this simple plastic bottle can teach them about current electricity. Invite any students who answer affirmatively to explain how.

STUDENT ACTIVITY
Pass out the squeeze bottles and, if possible, take your class to a grassy area outside. Explain to students that parts of their bottle will represent the electrical concepts of current, resistance, and voltage:

The rate of flow of water out of the bottle represents the rate of flow of electrons, or current.

The nozzle represents the resistance. Opening the nozzle decreases the resistance to the water flow. Pushing the nozzle closed increases it.

The pressure you put on the bottle—how hard you squeeze—represents the voltage. As you squeeze the bottle harder, the voltage increases. If you squeeze the bottle slightly, the voltage decreases.

The bottle itself represents the relationship between voltage, current, and resistance.

Have students use the squeeze-bottle model to answer these questions:

• *When you increase the voltage (push with greater force), what happens to the current?*

• *When you decrease the voltage (push with less force), what happens to the current?*

• *When you increase the resistance (close the top partially), what happens to the current?*

• *When you decrease the resistance (open the top completely), what happens to the current?*

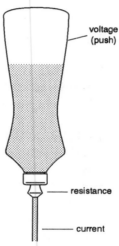

Now have students use their squeeze-bottle model to test out the relationship expressed in these statements:

• Increasing the voltage increases the electron flow.

• Decreasing the voltage decreases the electron flow.

• Increasing the resistance decreases the electron flow.

• Decreasing the resistance increases the electron flow.

If students are unsure of these concepts, have them refill the bottles and give them more time to experiment.

MAKING CONNECTIONS

Test for understanding by using these questions as a basis for discussion:

• *If the voltage in a circuit increases, what happens to the current (electron flow)?* (It increases.)

• *If the voltage in a circuit decreases, what happens to the current?* (It decreases.)

• *If the resistance in a circuit increases, what happens to the current?* (It decreases.)

• *If the resistance in a circuit decreases, what happens to the current?* (It increases.)

FOR FURTHER INVESTIGATION

Depending on the ability level of your students, you may want to introduce the Ohm's law equation, which mathematically describes the squeeze-bottle model.

What the squeeze-bottle model shows us is essentially what Georg Simon Ohm knew in 1827, when he announced the law that bears his name. See the *History* section and convey that information to students now.

Next, explain Ohm's law in the following way: Ohm said that

$$I = E/R$$

where I = current (or rate of electron flow expressed in amperes); E = voltage (expressed in volts); and R = resistance (expressed in ohms).

By plugging numbers into this formula, it is easy to demonstrate how Ohm's law describes the squeeze-bottle model.

• Suppose E = 1 volt and R = 1 ohm. Ohm's law tells us that E/R = 1 volt/1 ohm = I = 1 ampere, or amp.

Think of a stream of water from the squeeze bottle with the nozzle open and medium pressure applied.

• Now, increase the voltage to 10 volts. Ohm's law tells us that the electron flow is 10 times as great. E/R = 10 volts/1 ohm = I = 10 amps.

Imagine pressing as hard as you can on the squeeze bottle, increasing the water stream dramatically.

• Now, increase the resistance to 2 ohms. Ohm's law tells that the electron flow is halved. E/R = 10 volts/2 ohms = I = 5 amps.

Model this by closing the nozzle halfway. Again, press hard on the bottle. The water stream should be only a fraction of what it was with low resistance.

Now ask students to use Ohm's law to calculate these two problems:

1. Find the electron flow in a circuit with a 9-volt battery and a total resistance of 6 ohms. (Solution: I = E/R, so I = 9 volts/6 ohms = 1.5 amps.)

2. In order to light, a certain light bulb needs a current of 1 amp. If the circuit's resistance is 10 ohms, what voltage must be applied to the circuit? (Solution: By Ohm's law, we know that I = E/R. Therefore, 1 amp = E /10 ohms. E must equal 10 volts.)

HISTORY

Georg Simon Ohm systematically investigated the relationship between current, resistance, and voltage. In 1827 he expressed the relationship in an elegantly simple formula: I = E/R. The ohm, unit of resistance, was named in his honor. Unlike us, Ohm did not have the convenient electronic measuring devices of today. So his accomplishment is all the more impressive.

Electromagnetism

This unit deals with the development of two concepts and their technological applications: that an electron flow creates a magnetic force, and that a changing magnetic field causes electrons to flow. These concepts are two of the cornerstones of our modern technological infrastructure.

It is very easy for students to discover that a current produces a magnetic force: By causing a current to flow through a wire, they can see that a nearby compass needle is deflected. This simple phenomenon has found a wide variety of applications, from the electromagnet on the junkyard crane to the solenoid that pulls open the apartment-door lock to the common electric motor (which is essentially an electric magnet caused to spin via magnetic attraction and repulsion). If you are listening to music right now, it is probably being emitted from a speaker that contains a specialized electromagnet.

Experimentation leads students to observe that a changing magnetic field produces a current—a phenomenon known as electromagnetic induction—which also has a wide variety of applications. Two of these involve the generator and the transformer. Generators produce the current that flows into your light bulbs and the current that charges your car. Transformers are an essential part of your television, radio, microwave, stereo, computer, or almost anything that uses household current.

As the final project in this unit, students create their own example of radio waves, or electromagnetic radiation. Electromagnetic radiation is a changing magnetic field that produces an electric field and a changing electric field that produces a magnetic field. Although we cannot expect middle school students to be able to fully explain how radio waves are propagated through space (a topic reserved for high-school physics class), after reaching this point in the book, they may well be able to explain a part of the phenomenon.

The Great Magnetic Discovery

Magnetism from Electricity

Time **Thirty minutes**

MATERIALS

For each small group of students:

1 6-volt lantern battery (or 2 D-cells connected in parallel)

1-2 test leads (or 1 1' piece of copper wire, insulated or bare)

1 magnetic compass—not liquid-filled (cheap, lightweight compasses work best)

1 tbs iron filings (or steel wool)

3' of magnet wire

1 small funnel

OVERVIEW

Students will discover that electric current produces a magnetic force.

TEACHER BACKGROUND

Electric current—the flow of electrons—produces a magnetic force. It is this magnetic force that provides the electric power for almost every electrical device you can think of—television, radio, hair dryer, clock, typewriter, vacuum cleaner, air conditioner, circuit breaker, computer.

LAUNCHING THE LESSON

After distributing the materials, ask students what they know about magnetism and how it might be related to electricity. Then ask students for their comments and questions as you talk about the following properties of the materials:

• The compass needle is made of a magnet, which spins freely on a pivot. When the needle is in the presence of another magnetic force, it reacts by pivoting.

• The wire is made of copper and plastic insulation, which has no effect on the compass needle. When the hookup wire is attached to the terminals of the battery to make a closed circuit, electrons flow through the wire.

Explain that these materials are similar to those used in 1820 by Hans Oersted, a scientist who wanted to answer the important question *Is there any relationship between electricity and magnetism?* Challenge students to use the materials set before them to determine for themselves if there is a relationship between electricity and magnetism.

Try to avoid giving any further directions or hints for the time being. It is quite likely that some groups will be able to figure out how to investigate this problem. They can share their procedure and results with the other students. If only one group discovers the relationship between electricity and magnetism, have those students demonstrate for the rest of the class. If none of the groups discover this relationship, ask students to follow along as you present the process described in the *Student Activity* section.

STUDENT ACTIVITY

Following are the steps for using the relationship between magnetism and electricity:

1. Lay the compass on a tabletop. Wait for the compass needle to stop moving.

2. Place the middle of the test-lead wire directly over the compass needle. The wire should be perfectly parallel to the needle.

3. Open and close the circuit by connecting and disconnecting one of the alligator clips to and from one of the terminals. What do you see? (The compass needle will move. When the circuit is closed, the needle will align itself perpendicular to the wire. Then, when the circuit is opened, the needle will swing back to its original position.)

You may also wish to offer students the opportunity to test for the presence of a magnetic force without the use of a compass. If so, give them directions for one or both of the following activities:

4. Place iron filings or cut-up strands of fine steel wool around a length of wire connected to a lantern battery. Observe what happens to the iron filings when you open and close the circuit.

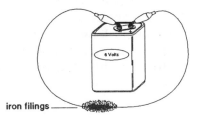

iron filings

5. Wind a length of magnet wire onto a small cone such as a funnel, leaving 2 feet of extra wire on each end. Remove the wire and flatten it into a coil. Then strip the insulation from the ends of the magnet wire and connect the ends of the wire to the terminals of a lantern battery. Suspend the coil loosely between two desks.

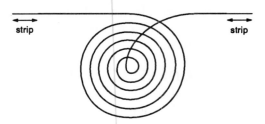

Hold one pole of a strong permanent magnet near the spiral coil. Open and close the circuit repeatedly to make the spiral swing back and forth. Depending on its orientation, the spiral will be attracted to, or repelled by, the magnet.

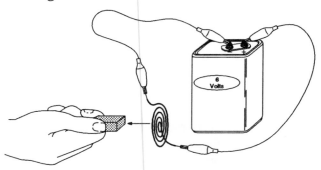

MAKING CONNECTIONS
Focus the discussion by asking questions such as these:
• *What is a magnetic compass made of?* (The needle of a compass is a small magnet. This magnet is allowed to spin freely.)
• *What can make the compass needle move?* (the magnetic force from another magnet, or an iron object)
• *Why did the compass needle move when a current began to flow through the wire near the needle?* (Answers should include a recognition that the current somehow produces a magnetic force.)

To complete the discussion, share the information provided about Hans Oersted in the *History* section.

FOR FURTHER INVESTIGATION
The following activity can be done by the whole class or by students working in small groups:

• Make a galvanometer, a sensitive device for detecting an electron flow. Place a compass on a piece of cardboard cut 2 centimeters wider and 8-10 centimeters longer than the compass diameter. Wrap 20 to 30 turns of magnet wire tightly around the compass and cardboard, leaving about 15 centimeters of extra wire at each end. Secure the windings with clear tape.

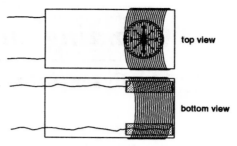

Push brass fasteners through the cardboard about 2 centimeters from the end. Strip the last 3 centimeters of each wire and wrap them around the paper fastener. Spread the leaves of the fastener apart and tape them in place.

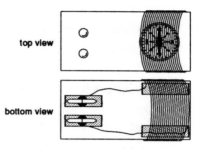

Place the galvanometer on a table-top and rotate it until the compass needle is parallel to the wire windings. Connect a 6-volt battery to the leads (paper fasteners) and see what happens to the compass needle.

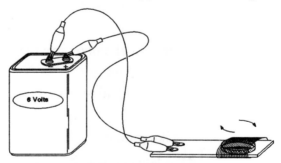

After doing this activity, students will know that the galvanometer works and can be used to test for electric currents. Beyond this, they may be surprised at how sensitive the galvanometer is.

HISTORY

In 1820, Hans Christian Oersted discovered the link between magnetism and electricity that he and many others had long suspected. The scientist did so in a simple experiment almost identical to the one in the *Student Activity* section that uses only a voltaic battery, a wire, and a magnetic compass. Oersted's discovery opened a floodgate of invention and further discovery. The creation of the electromagnet, electric motor, generator, and transformer all followed within 11 years!

·23· *Winding an Electromagnet*

An Essential Hands-On Experience

Time **One period**

MATERIALS

For each student or small group of students:

1 steel bolt, ⅜" diameter, 1½" length*

1 ⅜" nut (cheapest, nonhardened variety without radial lines, often called Grade 0)*

2 ⁵⁄₁₆" washers (must slide onto the ⅜" bolt)*

1 20-gauge magnet wire with enamel insulation approximately 40' long (Enamel type H-APTZ works well.)*

1 piece of fine or medium-coarse emery cloth approximately 1" x 2"*

1 lantern battery*

1-2 feet of plastic electrician's tape*

1 pair of scissors*

2 test leads*

1 large steel nail or any nonhardened steel object*

2 ⅜" washers

1 22- to 28-gauge magnet wire

2-4 D-cells

masking tape

*For teacher also

OVERVIEW

Students will use enameled magnet wire to construct small, powerful electromagnets.

TEACHER BACKGROUND

Winding an electromagnet is one of those classic science activities that no student should miss. Following the steps in the *Student Activity* section, students can construct small but powerful electromagnets, which they can later use to construct telegraphs, buzzers, speakers, and other projects. Why is the electromagnet as strong as it is? There are two reasons. The first has to do with magnet wire. Many windings of wire are wrapped around the magnet's core. Each winding of wire contributes to the overall magnetic force. The second and more important reason for the magnet's strength has to do with its iron core. Iron contains tiny magnetic domains—tiny regions of permanent magnetism distributed throughout the iron. Normally, these magnetic domains are oriented in random fashion so that their overall magnetic effect is zero. But under the influence of the external magnetic field provided when current flows through the coil of wire, the magnetic domains tend to line up in the same direction as the external field. Thus, the iron core turns into a strong temporary magnet.

LAUNCHING THE LESSON

Ask students to imagine a junkyard where an enormous electromagnet hangs from the boom of a large crane. The crane drops the magnet on top of an old car. The magnet turns on and grabs the car. Then both magnet and car are lifted into the air and swung over the scrap heap, where the electromagnet turns off and the car falls. Tell students that they will now make their own small versions of this junkyard electromagnet.

STUDENT ACTIVITY

Distribute materials to students in their groups. Demonstrate each step as you direct students to build their electromagnets as follows:

1. Place the two washers on the bolt, and screw on the nut until it is even with the end of the bolt. Wrap the exposed threads of the bolt with one or two layers of tape to prevent the threads from cutting the wire.

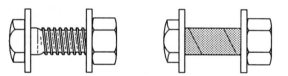

2. Begin winding the magnet wire around the bolt between the two washers. Be sure to leave 1 foot of extra wire at the beginning. Do not wind the end of the wire onto the bolt.

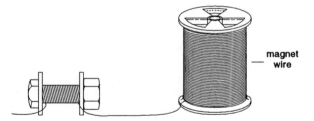

magnet wire

Wrap carefully from one end of the bolt to the other and back again. Keep wrapping until the wire is wound to the outer circumference of the washers. Cut the magnet wire from the spool, leaving 1 foot of extra wire.

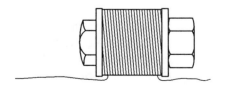

3. Wrap the coiled wire with two layers of tape. Pull the tape tight so that the wire will not unwind.

4. Use emery cloth to strip the last 2-3 centimeters of the ends of the magnet wire. Fold the emery cloth around the end of the wire and pull with a squeezing motion. Three or four passes should strip the enamel on two sides.

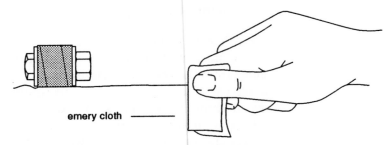

emery cloth —————

5. Turn the wire 90 degrees and repeat the stripping motion. When the wire is completely bare, it will have a light copper color.

6. Use test leads to connect the electromagnet to the lantern battery. Test the magnet's pulling power with scissors, paper clips, or any steel object.

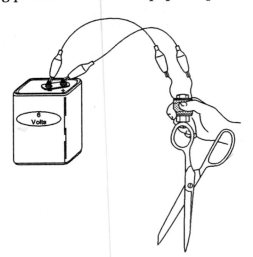

CAUTION

If students are using a fresh lantern battery, the magnet may heat up quickly. Disconnect the magnet periodically to let it cool.

MAKING CONNECTIONS

Have students gather together to share their observations and consider the following questions:

• *What practical uses can you think of for an electromagnet?*

• *Do the electrons have to be moving through the wire for the magnet to be on?* (Yes.)

• *Would the magnet work if there were no insulation on the magnet wires?* (No, for the electrons would take the shortest path—skipping sideways from wire to wire. The insulation forces the electrons to take the long path, around and around, through the whole coil.)

path, around and around, through the whole coil.)

FOR FURTHER INVESTIGATION

Using the electromagnet students have assembled, invite them to try any of the following activities:

• Determine if the electromagnet has poles and whether they change with changes in the direction of electron flow. If the direction of electron flow changes, do the poles change? (Students should find that there are poles and that the orientation of these poles is determined by the direction of the electron flow.)

• Investigate the electromagnet's lines of magnetic force with steel wool or iron filings. Lay the electromagnet on its side and cover it with a piece of cardboard or stiff paper. Connect the electromagnet to the battery to turn it on. Sprinkle tiny bits of steel—which you can prepare by cutting an old steel-wool pad with scissors—on top of the cardboard. (Students should find that it forms an interesting pattern.) Turn the electromagnet on and off and you will see the lines of magnetic force rising and falling.

• Hold an electromagnet lifting contest. How many paper clips, washers, or bolts can your electromagnet lift at once? How can the electromagnet be made stronger?

• Wind a solenoid, which is a sucking electromagnet. Cut a 10-centimeter section from a drinking straw. Wind two layers of magnet wire up and down its length, leaving a foot of extra wire on each end. Strip the wire ends and connect them to a lantern battery. Unfold a small steel paper clip and insert it into bottom of the straw. The solenoid should suck the paper clip inside.

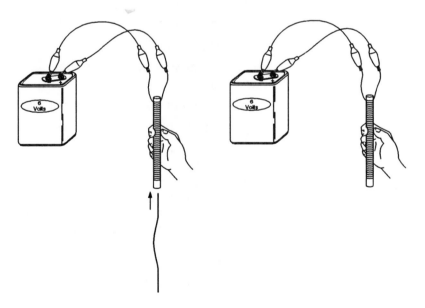

The Box Buzzer and Telegraph

Using the Electromagnet

Time **One or two periods**

MATERIALS

For each small group of students:

l electromagnet*

1 hacksaw blade (or 1 steel knife or spatula)*

1-2 lantern batteries (or 1 dc power supply)*

1 small paper clip (or 1 large paper clip)*

3 test leads*

1-2 small pieces of emery cloth (or 1-2 small plain pieces of steel wool torn from a pad or 1 soaped steel wool pad with soap rinsed out and dried)*

1 roll of masking tape*

1 pair of scissors*

1 cardboard box*

1 cardboard piece about 5 cm x 10 cm

1 medium paper clip

2 bare copper wires approximately 20 gauge, each 10 cm long (or magnet wire with the ends stripped)

2 brass fasteners (or 2 thin strips of aluminum foil)

low voltage dc power supply (optional)

*For teacher also

OVERVIEW

Students will use their electromagnets to construct simple buzzer circuits. They will then adapt the buzzer circuit to make a telegraph. Students can use this device to send messages in Morse code.

TEACHER BACKGROUND

At the core of the old-fashioned electric bell that rings between classes at school, and the old telephone at home, is the buzzer, a circuit that repeatedly turns itself on and off. This circuit is designed so that current flows through a steel blade. An electromagnet, positioned nearby, pulls the steel blade back. This opens the circuit—meaning it stops the current from flowing—and this turns the electromagnet off. When the electromagnet is off, the steel blade springs back into position, closing the circuit and allowing current to flow. Now the electromagnet is on again, so it pulls the steel blade back. This process keeps repeating itself: The steel blade swings back and forth, usually fast enough to create an audible tone. (A vibration faster than 20 per second and slower than about 20,000 per second is interpreted by our brains as a tone.)

In this lesson, students will create an inexpensive version of that cleverly devised circuit. Using only a electromagnet, an empty cardboard box, and a saw blade, students can put together a working buzzer in minutes.

PREPARATION

Follow the directions in the *Student Activity* section to construct your own buzzer prior to the lesson so that students may refer to it as a model when building their own.

LAUNCHING THE LESSON

Demonstrate your homemade buzzer and explain that this is another example of a clever use for the electromagnet. Mention that before the onset of electronic sirens and beepers, the buzzer was commonly found in doorbells, car horns, fire alarms, and any other objects where ringing or buzzing was required. Tell students that they will work in groups to make first a buzzer and then a telegraph.

STUDENT ACTIVITY

Distribute materials to each group. Direct students to construct and use the buzzer as follows:

1. Use emery cloth to scrub the paint or clear protective coating from the last 2 centimeters of both sides of the hacksaw blade.

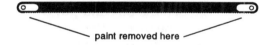

paint removed here

2. Strip the last 2 inches of one lead of the electromagnet. Wind this stripped end around the unpainted end of the hacksaw blade. Tape the wire firmly against the blade.

3. Use scissors to cut a small opening in the edge of the cardboard box as shown below. Insert a paper clip into the opening. The small loop of the paper clip should be on the inside of the box and the large loop on the outside.

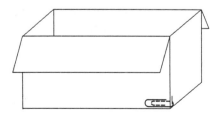

4. Tape the saw blade to the side of the box so that the stripped end of the blade is held lightly against the paper clip. It should be easy to bend the saw blade back from the paper clip.

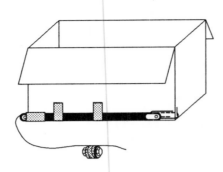

5. Tape the electromagnet firmly onto the work surface.

6. Complete the circuit with two test leads. One wire should connect the paper clip from the inside of the box to one of the battery's terminals. The other wire should connect the free lead of the electromagnet to the other terminal.

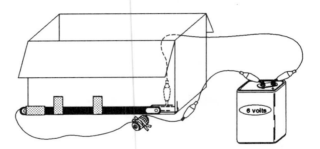

7. Open the box and put two or three textbooks inside to weight it down. Slide the box so that the end of the saw blade is close to the electromagnet. At this point, the blade should begin to vibrate, and you should hear a buzz. Adjust the position of the box to make the buzzing as loud as possible.

CAUTION
The electromagnet and paper clip may get very hot.

Now give students directions for constructing a switch to convert their buzzer into a telegraph:

8. Partially unbend a paper clip.

9. Use a brass fastener to attach the small loop of the paper clip to the cardboard. Put another brass fastener through the cardboard so that it lies underneath the large loop of the paper clip.

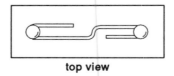

top view

10. Wind a piece of bare copper wire around the legs of one of the brass fasteners and then press down the legs. Repeat this procedure for the other fastener.

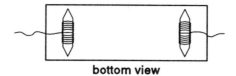

bottom view

11. Place the switch in the buzzer circuit. Depress the switch and see what happens. (When the switch is depressed, electrons flow through the circuit, and the buzzer buzzes. Releasing the switch stops the buzzing.)

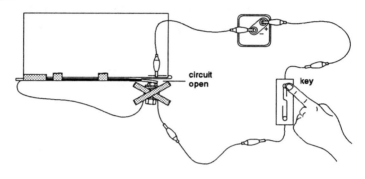

circuit open

key

CAUTION
The paper clip may get hot.

Troubleshooting

If the buzzer won't buzz, check for the following:

• *The battery is too weak.* It may be necessary to connect two or even three batteries in series, positive to negative. You could also try substituting a plug-in, low-voltage dc power supply.

• *The blade saw doesn't make contact with the paper clip.* Retape as necessary.

• *The saw blade is held too tightly against the box.* Retape so that the blade can vibrate more easily.

MAKING CONNECTIONS

Challenge students to analyze the buzzer and to explain why the buzzer buzzes. To facilitate the discussion, introduce the terms *circuit*, *closed circuit*, and *open circuit*. A circuit is essentially a path along which electrons can flow. If the path is continuous from the negative to the positive terminals of a battery, the circuit is said to be closed. If the path is not continuous—there is a break or opening at some point—the circuit is open. If necessary, ask questions to guide students toward understanding the following specific details:

• Because the hacksaw blade is made of steel, the electromagnet is able to pull it back away from the paper clip. As the blade is pulled back, the circuit is opened. So the electrons stop flowing through the electromagnet, and the magnet turns off.

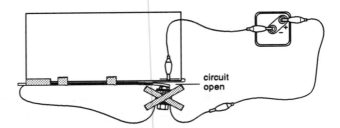

circuit open

• Because electrons are not flowing through it, the electromagnet loses its power, and the hacksaw blade springs into its original position against the paper clip. The circuit begins to close again and electrons again begin to flow.

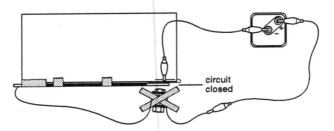

circuit closed

• The whole process repeats itself again and again as the blade travels back and forth from magnet to clip, several times per second. This vibration produces the buzzing sound.

FOR FURTHER INVESTIGATION

If you like, allow students to use their telegraphs to send messages in Morse code. Duplicate and distribute the following diagram for students' use.

International Morse Code

A	• ▬		N	▬ •
B	▬ • • •		O	▬ ▬ ▬
C	▬ • ▬ •		P	• ▬ ▬ •
D	▬ • •		Q	▬ ▬ • ▬
E	•		R	• ▬ •
F	• • ▬ •		S	• • •
G	▬ ▬ •		T	▬
H	• • • •		U	• • ▬
I	• •		V	• • • ▬
J	• ▬ ▬ ▬		W	• ▬ ▬
K	▬ • ▬		X	▬ • • ▬
L	• ▬ • •		Y	▬ • ▬ ▬
M	▬ ▬		Z	▬ ▬ • •

Explain that each dot is represented by a short buzz, each dash by a long buzz, and the buzz for the dash is three times as long as that for the dot. Using Morse code takes some practice, but it is a good deal of fun.

HISTORY

Popular history holds that Samuel B. Morse invented the first telegraph. What he really deserves credit for is inventing the first simple telegraph code and establishing the first commercially successful telegraph system. However, he was by no means the first to conceive of communicating over long distances by transmitting electrical impulses. One of the most notable first attempts involved 26 different wires, one for each letter of the alphabet! An operator at the transmitting end would send a current through one wire at a time. Then, at the receiving end, another operator would look for bubbles formed. These bubbles indicated that a current was flowing through that wire.

By the mid-1830s, the telegraph was an idea whose time had finally come. Morse, an artist with no training in electricity, was the one to pursue the idea. He devised the now-famous Morse code, in which each letter was assigned a unique combination of dots and dashes. At first, Morse's telegraph was designed to write dots and dashes on paper that was rolled beneath a pencil attached to an iron spring. Soon, however, telegraph operators learned to decode the messages by sound, and the paper was abandoned altogether.

·25· *The Juice-Can Speaker*

A Real Speaker from an Orange-Juice Can

Time **One period**

MATERIALS

The following materials are needed for you to demonstrate the building of one speaker. If you want to have students, working in small groups, make a speaker, provide one set of the following for each group:

1 electromagnet

1 strong permanent magnet (not a horseshoe magnet)

1 frozen orange-juice can

1 steel wastepaper basket (optional)

1 radio (or 1 stereo receiver or tape player)

2 test leads

OVERVIEW

Either you will demonstrate to students how to construct a working speaker out of a frozen orange-juice can, a permanent magnet, and an electromagnet, or students will make their own. If students do make the speakers, they will use a metal wastepaper basket in place of the juice can.

TEACHER BACKGROUND

When you drop a permanent magnet inside an orange-juice can, the can becomes one part of a homemade speaker. Then, by holding an electromagnet near the can, you create a working speaker that has surprisingly good clarity. This is a wonderful way to learn how an electromagnetic speaker works.

The radio amplifier sends a current to the electromagnet, and the current changes according to the pattern of sound to be reproduced. The magnet's pull on the can varies according to the changing current. The can vibrates according to the pull of the electromagnet, so the sound emerges from the can in the form of vibrating columns of air.

You can also substitute a steel wastepaper basket or any steel-bottomed container for the juice can in order to make a working speaker. The wastepaper basket makes a wonderful speaker that vibrates all around a head that is put inside!

PREPARATION

Disconnect the speakers from your radio. If you have a component system, this is simply a matter of removing the speaker wire from the back of the speaker.

If you have a portable radio, make sure the radio is not plugged in. Then, remove the screws and take off the cover. Locate the wires to the speakers and try to unplug them from the amplifier (often this is easy to do). If you can't do this, cut the speaker wire instead and strip both ends of each of the wires that you cut. (You can twist the wires back together again when you are done, returning your radio to working condition.) If possible, snap the radio's case back together, leaving the two speaker wires outside. You will hook your homemade speaker to these wires.

Wash out a metal wastepaper basket. Have your permanent magnet available.

LAUNCHING THE LESSON

Tell students that by the end of the lesson, they will ask to put their heads inside a wastepaper basket! Students will, of course, deny that they would ever do such a thing.

STUDENT ACTIVITY

Either have students assist you in making a speaker or give the following directions for students to make speakers:

1. Place the permanent magnet in the bottom of the orange-juice can so that one pole touches the bottom.

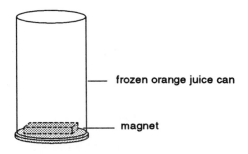

frozen orange juice can

magnet

2. Attach the leads of your electromagnet to the speaker wire of the radio. Turn on the radio to top volume and tune it in to a station.

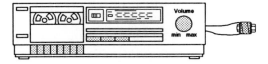

3. Hold the orange-juice can to your ear. Slowly bring the electromagnet to the back of the can and describe what you hear.

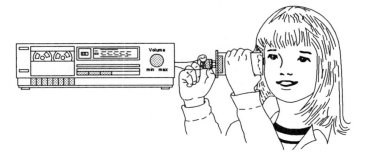

4. Now replace the orange-juice can with a metal wastepaper basket.

5. Take turns putting heads in the wastepaper basket and describe what you hear. What other metal objects might you use to make speakers?

Students could also substitute a large steel can from the school cafeteria for the juice can. Even a metal desk can be made into a speaker by putting the permanent magnet on one of the sides of the desk and holding the electromagnet on the reverse of that side.

MAKING CONNECTIONS

Ask students to explain how the speaker reproduces the sound. Here is information that you might want to share with the students:

• The radio sends an electron flow through the speaker wires that flows according to the sound it recreates. For example, suppose the radio plays a piano's A note. The original, recorded A string vibrated 440 times per second. The radio recreates that sound by sending an electron flow to the speaker. This flow changes 440 times per second—that is, the electromagnet is turned on and off 440 times per second. This causes the orange-juice can, or any steel container, to be pulled and released 440 times per second, producing the vibrations that make an A tone in your ear.

• Students often suspect that sound waves are piped through the wires from the radio to the speaker. There are at least two ways you can show them that this is not true. First, tell students to hold the speaker wires while the radio is playing. If sound waves were traveling through the wires, students would feel the vibrations of the low notes with their hands. But they won't feel any vibrations at all. Second, replace the speaker wires with rubber tubing. Invite students to put the rubber tubing into their ears. No sound waves will be detected. What will pass through the wires between the radio and the speaker is only a rapidly changing electric current.

FOR FURTHER INVESTIGATION

Suggest that students work on the following activities in groups or on their own:

• Make different kinds of speakers. What other objects can you use in place of the orange-juice can and the wastepaper basket? Try any flat steel object. Would a wooden tabletop work? How many unique ways can you discover to make a speaker?

• Use more than one juice can to make a speaker. Would two or three cans and just one magnet work?

• Take apart a commercially made speaker. Try to identify the parts of this speaker that are similar to the parts of the juice-can speaker.

HISTORY

The speaker came into existence as part of the telephone. Alexander Graham Bell used a speaker similar to ours in his first systems. Electromagnetic speakers have been in use continuously since then, with few major design changes.

·26· Electricity from Magnetism

Generating an Electron Flow

Time **Thirty minutes**

MATERIALS

The following materials are needed for you or for each small group of students to demonstrate electromagnetic induction:

1 electromagnet

1 strong permanent magnet—such as a Radio Shack #64-1877—(or 1 electromagnet

2 test leads

1 compass galvanometer—directions for constructing galvanometers are found in the *For Further Investigation* section of Lesson 22 of this unit (or 1 magnetic compass—not liquid-filled, magnet wire, emery cloth, tape)

OVERVIEW

Either you or your students will use a permanent magnet and an electromagnet to generate an electron flow.

TEACHER BACKGROUND

That electricity and magnetism are related became clear in Lesson 22, when we saw that an electron flow produced a magnetic force. But can a magnetic force produce an electron flow? Absolutely. This phenomenon is easily demonstrated with simple equipment.

Electromagnetic induction, a fancy name for using a moving magnetic force to produce an electron flow, is not an esoteric phenomenon. Generators in electric-power plants are essentially scaled-up versions of the activity that follows, in which a coil of wire passes through a magnetic field.

PREPARATION

If students didn't make galvanometers in Lesson 22, give them the following directions for making these instruments during the period preceding the actual lesson:

• Use a 1' piece of magnet wire. Wrap the wire around the compass. Strip the ends of the wire with a piece of emery cloth. Align the compass so that the needle is parallel to the wires, and tape it to your work surface. (See the illustration on the next page.)

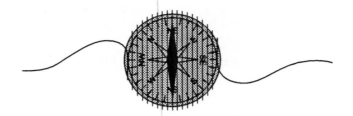

LAUNCHING THE LESSON

Turn the classroom lights on and then off. Ask students what makes the current flow through the lights. Some may realize that electric power is produced in a centralized power plant. Some may even have heard that the local power plant burns coal or runs on nuclear fuel or whatever the case may be.

Ask students exactly what it is inside the power plant that actually makes a current flow. A big battery? A large static-charge machine and a huge capacitor? Tell students that in this lesson they will learn to produce a current by the same method that almost all power stations use—electromagnetic induction. This phenomenon is complicated but easy to show.

STUDENT ACTIVITY

Either have students work with you on a demonstration or give the following directions for small groups of students to make electromagnetic induction:

1. Use hookup wires to attach the galvanometer (the wire-and-compass you constructed). Stretch out the wires so that the electromagnet is as far as possible from the compass.

2. With a quick motion, swing one pole of the permanent magnet by the electromagnet. You should see a slight movement of the compass needle.

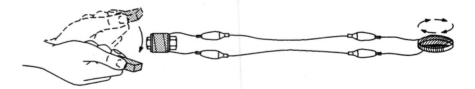

Remember, the movement of the compass needle means that electrons are flowing through the wires.

3. Pass the permanent magnet repeatedly past the electromagnet to cause the compass needle to swing widely.

4. Now try keeping the permanent magnet near the electromagnet but perfectly still. What do you notice? (Students will see that the compass needle doesn't move as long as the permanent magnet isn't moving.)

MAKING CONNECTIONS

Use these questions to guide students in a discussion about their observations and speculations:

• *What does the movement of the compass needle mean?* (Electrons are flowing through the wires that surround it.)

• *What happens to the compass needle when the permanent magnet is lying still near the electromagnet?* (It remains still. The compass needle moves only when the permanent magnet is moving near the electromagnet.)

• *When the compass needle moves, electrons must be flowing through the circuit. Where does the electron flow come from if there is no battery in the circuit?* (In essence, as the permanent magnet moves past the coil of wire in the electromagnet, its lines of magnetic force—or magnetic field—pass through the coil of wire. As they do so, these lines of magnetic force push electrons through the wire.)

Pause in the discussion to help students understand these concepts by offering this analogy: Imagine that an electron is like a steel ball called a BB. You can place the BB on top of a table and hold a magnet underneath. When you move the magnet under the table, the steel ball moves with it. But when the magnet is held still, the BB does not move. The magnetic force is able to pass through the wooden tabletop just as the magnetic force can pass through the insulation and copper of a wire.

Now imagine a hula hoop completely filled with steel BBs. The hula hoop is like the wire in our circuit, and the BBs are the electrons within it. The permanent magnet's lines of magnetic force can pull the BBs around the hula hoop. Moving the BBs at one point in the hula hoop instantly makes all of the others move around the hula hoop too. The BBs that flow when the magnet moves are already present in the hula hoop. No extra BBs are added to the system.

Who can recall what the term electromagnetic induction means? How does it relate to what we just did? (Students may remember that it is what happens when a magnetic field moves across a wire and electrons are made to flow.)

FOR FURTHER INVESTIGATION

Try some of these activities with your students:

• Repeat the above activity substituting a second electromagnet for the permanent magnet. Use hookup wires to connect the second electromagnet to a 6-volt battery and swing the second electromagnet past the first electromagnet. Again, you should see the needle jiggle, indicating an electron flow.

• Place the two electromagnets on top of each other. Quickly connect the second electromagnet to the lantern battery and then quickly disconnect it. Again, the compass needle jiggles, indicating an electron flow. Why?

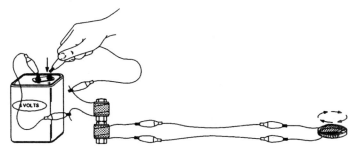

(When an electromagnet is turned on and off and on, one is causing the electromagnet's lines of magnetic force to rise and collapse, the second to move. Look back at the *For Further Investigation* section of Lesson 23 for directions about what to observe as the lines of magnetic force rise and collapse.)

• Take apart an inexpensive handcrank generator and you will find coils of magnet wire. These are basically one or more electromagnets rotating within two semicylindrical permanent magnets.

HISTORY

Michael Faraday, one of the great experimental scientists of the nineteenth century, reasoned that an electron flow in one direction might create an electron flow in the opposite direction in a nearby conductor. Faraday tried, unsuccessfully, to produce this effect. What he did find, however, was that at the precise moment that he closed or opened the circuit, an electron flow was induced. It was the variation in the electron flow of the primary circuit, he discovered, that induced the electron flow in the secondary circuit.

·27· An Incredible Shock

Using a Transformer

Time **Thirty minutes**

MATERIALS

For each student or small group of students:

1 "step-down" power transformer—such as Radio Shack #273-1352—(or 1 transformer from a broken radio)*

1 weak (used) AA-cell*

Items needed for the demonstration in the *Making Connections* section:

1 6-volt battery

5 steel paper clips

*For teacher also

OVERVIEW

Students will experiment to determine that a 1.5-volt current turned on and off repeatedly can be raised by a transformer to become a 15-volt shock. Safety procedures must be strictly adhered to.

TEACHER BACKGROUND

You may think that a dead AA flashlight cell is incapable of giving a shock. But a transformer has the remarkable ability to change the low voltage current from an apparently dead AA-cell to a higher-voltage shock. And, in its more common use, a transformer can change the high voltage from a wall outlet to a gentler, lower-voltage current for use in a radio, computer, or other electronic device. Yet this highly useful device is supremely simple—essentially just two electromagnets, one on top of the other.

This experiment may well become one of your students' favorites. Students may even salvage their own transformers from broken radios or video games.

PREPARATION

It is important that you test the AA-cells on yourself to make sure they are nearly dead before allowing students to use them. Enlist an adult helper to follow the directions in the *Student Activity* section so that you can sample the resulting shock. Be sure to use the one-hand safety technique. If the cell is fresh, the shock may be unpleasant. But if the cell is suitably used up—nearly dead—the shock will be mild. You can deaden a cell by connecting a wire from the positive to the negative terminal overnight.

LAUNCHING THE LESSON

Pass around a used AA-cell and describe it as "used up." Tell students that they will have a chance to use a transformer to make the AA-cell shock even though it is nearly dead. Describe the shock as similar in intensity to that produced by the capacitor. Do not allow students to begin the activity before you convey the following safety rules and check that all participants can comply:

SAFETY PROCEDURE

- The student who feels the shock should use one hand only. The other hand should be kept in a pocket or behind the back.
- Wear rubber-soled shoes, and the hands should be dry.
- Use only deadened AA-cells pretested and approved by your teacher.

STUDENT ACTIVITY

Distribute materials. Then display a transformer and invite students to explain what a transformer is and does. Help them to understand that it is a device for changing the voltage of an electric current. As students may recall from their experience with the voltaic pile, an increase in voltage usually results in an increase in shocking efficiency. Identify the two transformer wires that lead to the coil of thicker magnetic wire.

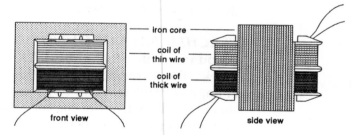

Now give students the following directions:

1. Pick up one of the two transformer wires leading to the thick coil and touch it to the negative end of the AA-cell.

2. Touch the other wire to the positive end of the cell in a light tickling motion. What do you see and feel? (Students may see tiny sparks and feel a very faint shock.)

Have a willing partner hold the other wire with one hand so that both bare wire ends touch the skin but do not touch each other.

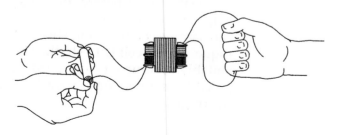

What does your partner feel at the moment you tickle the cell? (The person will feel a fairly mild shock.)

3. Stop tickling the cell and hold the wires steady on it. What do you feel at the other end? (Students should feel no shock. Help students to realize that it is only at the instant that they open or close the circuit that someone feels a shock.)

4. Reverse the coils so that you are tickling the leads from the coil with many turns of thin wire while your partner holds the leads from the coil of thick wire. What happens? (The transformer won't shock.)

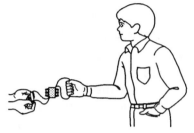

MAKING CONNECTIONS

To facilitate the discussion, explain the terms *primary circuit* and *secondary circuit*. The primary circuit of the transformer includes the 1.5-volt cell, the transformer coil with the fewer turns of thicker wire, and the connecting wires between coil and cell. The secondary circuit consists of both the other coil, which has many turns of very thin wire, and the body of the person who holds the ends of these wires to feel the shock.

CAUTION

This activity should be presented as a demonstration only. *Do not allow students to have access to the transformers and the 6-volt lantern batteries at the same time!* If students were to use the fresh 6-volt batteries as they did the AA-cells, they could receive a painful shock.

Ask students how the transformer is similar to an electromagnet. After they have shared their ideas, demonstrate that the transformer is essentially two electromagnets, one on top of the other. Do this by connecting the leads of one coil to a 6-volt battery. Hold the transformer in the air with one hand. With the other hand, touch a few small paper clips to the bottom of the transformer. The transformer will hold up the paper clips.

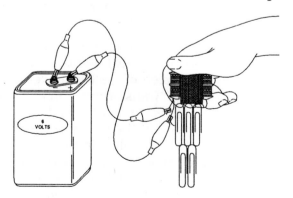

Have students consider the following questions:

• *If the transformer consists of 2 coils of wires isolated from each other, and electrons cannot pass directly from the primary circuit to the secondary circuit, does a current in the primary circuit create a current in the secondary circuit?* (Students may recall from the previous lesson that the answer lies in understanding that as the current in the primary circuit changes, the magnetic field around it changes. Each time you close the primary circuit by touching the leads to the AA-cell, lines of magnetic force essentially expand outward while the current is established. When you open the primary circuit, the lines of magnetic force collapse inward as the current stops. These moving lines of magnetic force cut across the secondary coil. Therefore, a current is produced in the secondary coil by electromagnetic induction.)

• *When you hold the wires on the ends of the AA-cell without letting go, why doesn't the transformer shock?* (A current is only induced in the secondary coil when the lines of magnetic force expand or contract. This happens only at those moments when the primary circuit is open or closed.)

Give students an opportunity to answer the next question before you share the information beneath it.

• *How does the transformer make a 1.5-volt cell shock?*

Concept 1: The transformer essentially makes a second current, with a higher or lower voltage, out of the current that you put into it. In this activity, the transformer steps up the voltage from 1.5 volts in the primary circuit to about 15 volts (more or less, depending on your transformer) in the secondary circuit.

Concept 2: The more the turns of wire in the secondary coil, the greater the voltage produced. Each turn of wire collects a certain amount of voltage from the moving lines of magnetic force. Thus, a secondary coil with many turns produces a higher voltage.

Concept 3: It is actually the ratio of the turns of the primary coil to the secondary coil that determines the factor by which the transformer multiplies or divides the voltage. For example, if there are 500 turns in the primary coil and 5,000 turns in the secondary, the factor is 10. Such a ratio would transform the 1.5 volt current of the AA-cell to 15 volts.

Concept 4: You do not get something for nothing. When a transformer steps up a voltage by a factor of 10, it simultaneously divides the current by the same factor. So, although voltage is increased, the current, or size of electron flow, is decreased.

Finally, give students a chance to think of ways that transformers are used in the real world. Together, establish that transformers are used in every step of electric-power delivery between the power plant and one's home. Transformers can either step up or step down voltage. Generators at a power plant typically produce an alternating current at 20,000 volts. Outside of the power plant, a transformer is used to step up the voltage to 400,000 volts. In this high-voltage state, the power can be transmitted over great distances with less loss to resistance. At the edge of a city or town, another large transformer steps the high-voltage current down to about 4,000 volts. Near one's house, another transformer steps the current down to 220 or 110 volts. This is the voltage available when someone plugs something into a wall socket.

FOR FURTHER INVESTIGATION

Students can do the following investigations on their own and report back to the class:

• Open up a portable radio or tape player. (It must be the kind you can plug into a wall outlet.) Look closely at the path the current takes, beginning from the plug end. You will find that the cord leads directly to the transformer. Can you explain why?

CAUTION

If a student is interested in pulling his or her own transformers from a broken radio, insist that the student do so either under your supervision or that of a parent. Advise the student to unplug the radio, with its power switch turned off, long before dismantling it. In addition, advise the use of insulated tools; capacitors within the radio can store a charge long after the radio has been unplugged. **Finally, dissuade students from dismantling a television, which contains a variety of hazards, including enormous capacitors that can store lethal charges.**

• Walk around your neighborhood and locate the transformers on telephone poles. If possible, visit the nearby substation where you can see the enormous transformers stepping down the 400,000-volt current.

• Find the ignition coil in an automobile. This is a special transformer designed to produce the terrific voltages needed to jump the gap in a spark plug. If possible, take an ignition coil apart. You will be amazed at the vast number of turns of superfine magnetic wire.

HISTORY

The invention of the transformer was one of the most important outgrowths of Michael Faraday's research into electromagnetic induction. It was found that the transformer could multiply or divide the input voltage of the primary circuit according to the ratio of primary to secondary windings.

Curiously, the United States Patent Office rejected the first patent application for a transformer in the 1880s on the grounds that the inventors claimed to have created power out of nothing. What they didn't realize was that the increase in voltage in the secondary coil was accompanied by a corresponding decrease in current so that the power out of the system was no greater than the power put into it.

·28· *Constructing a Tesla Coil*

A Homemade Air-Core Transformer

Time **One period**

MATERIALS
For each small group of students:

1 20-gauge magnet wire, 30 m (90′) long (or 1 18-gauge insulated wire of any type)*

1 16-gauge plastic insulated wire, 3 m (10′) long*

1 electrophorus*

4 hookup wires*

1 Leyden jar*

1 roll of masking tape (or 1 roll of tape of any kind)*

2 shiny pennies (or 2 coins or rounded metal objects)*

1 metric ruler*

1 cardboard paper-towel core (or 1 toilet-paper core or plastic or glass bottle; do not use steel or aluminum cans.)*

1 piece of emery cloth*

*For teacher also

OVERVIEW
Students will construct an air-core transformer to step up the voltage of a capacitor discharge, thereby developing an understanding of how the Tesla coil is constructed. They will then use these homemade transformers to create radio waves, as described in the next lesson.

TEACHER BACKGROUND
Nikola Tesla, famous for experiments with high-voltage currents, made great use of his Tesla coil, a transformer without an iron core. The air-core transformer is similar to a basic Tesla coil and can produce an arc of about 40,000 volts.

PREPARATION
Set up all the materials for making and using the coil so that you can demonstrate the steps for students as they do them.

LAUNCHING THE LESSON
Two of the most exciting "shockers" described in this book are the capacitor and the transformer. Tell students that the capacitor, when thoroughly charged, can produce 10,000 volts and that now you will

show them how to make a special transformer that can, theoretically, step up that voltage 10 times. Students will most likely find this prospect intriguing.

STUDENT ACTIVITY

Using the following directions, guide students in making and using the special transformer:

1. To make the transformer, wind 150 turns of magnet wire snugly around the middle of the paper-towel core. Wind each turn as neatly as possible, leaving no gaps in between. Leave 1 foot of extra magnet wire at each end. Use emery cloth to strip the last 2 to 3 centimeters of enamel from each end.

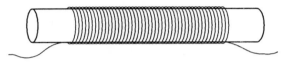

2. Neatly wrap the finished coil with masking tape.

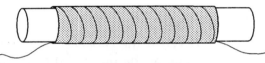

3. Wrap 15 turns of 16-gauge insulated wire on top of the masking tape, centering it on the inner coil. Leave 1 foot of extra wire at each end.

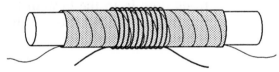

4. Wrap this insulated wire coil with masking tape and strip the plastic insulation from the last inch of each end.

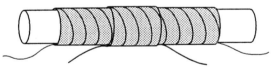

5. Shine two pennies with emery cloth and place them in alligator clips. Position the hookup wire so that the pennies are about .5 centimeters apart and even with each other. Connect the hookup wires to the inside coil on the paper-towel core.

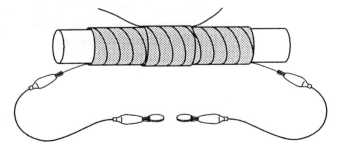

6. Now power your air-core transformer. Use an electrophorus to charge the capacitor 50 times.

Note: Remind students of safety rules.

To save time, you can ground the capacitor to the outer coil of the transformer.

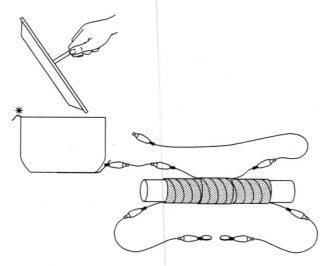

7. When the capacitor is charged, connect its ground lead to one of the leads of the outer coil of the air-core transformer and then turn off the lights. Touch the other wire of the outer coil to the top of the capacitor. This sends the capacitor's charge through the outer coil. Remember, electrons flow from the bottom foil, through the wire, to the top foil. Now watch the two pennies. What do you see between them? (Students should see a spark.)

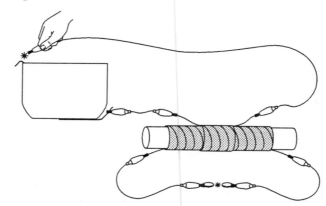

Once you have made the arc jump between the pennies, try separating the pennies further to see how far you can make the arc jump, recharge the capacitor, and try again.

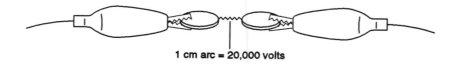

1 cm arc = 20,000 volts

MAKING CONNECTIONS

Help students to further understanding by discussing the following question:

• *If both the inside and the outside coils are coated with insulation, how does the inside coil get its charge?* (As the capacitor discharges, electrons flow through the outside coil and then quickly stop. The lines of magnetic force created by this momentary electron flow collapse when the electron flow stops. They push, or induce, an electron flow in the inside coil. Although electrons can't cross the insulation barrier, the magnetic force can.)

FOR FURTHER INVESTIGATION

Try this activity with your students:

• Students will enjoy combining art and electricity in "High Voltage Art." In addition to the equipment listed earlier in this lesson, groups will need a plastic or paper plate, aluminum foil, scissors, and glue. Cut 20 very small pieces of aluminum foil, approximately 5 millimeters square. Trace a simple pattern onto the plastic plate. Coat the pattern with a very thin layer of glue.

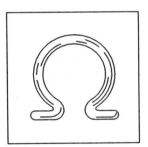

Place the squares on the glue, as close to one another as possible so that only a hair's width shows between each foil piece. As the final piece of each end of the design, glue a .5 centimeter x 10 centimeter foil piece to be used as a connector.

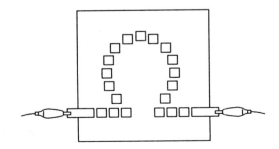

Use two hookup wires to attach the secondary coil of the air-core transformer to the foil-square pattern as shown. Charge the capacitor at least 20 times with the electrophorus.

CAUTION

Remember that the capacitor can deliver a nasty shock, so be careful. Discharge the capacitor through the primary coil of the air-core transformer.

With the lights out, students will see each gap between the aluminum pieces illuminated with a bright spot of light.

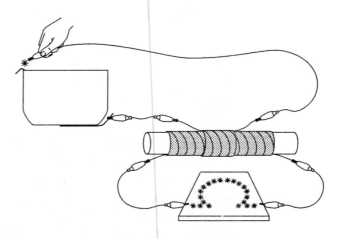

If you or a student cannot get the design to light, check for excessive glue, excessively large gaps between foil pieces, or too many foil pieces.

Talk over the following with students:

• *Why is it necessary to use the transformer to bridge the gaps between the aluminum pieces? Why can't the capacitor do it directly?* (The air-core transformer produces an electron flow with higher voltage. This high voltage is needed to jump the many air gaps between the foil pieces.)

• *Why is it necessary to limit the number and size of the gaps in the foil design?* (Too many gaps would mean too great a resistance, and the electrons would not be able to flow.)

The Birth of Radio

Produce and Detect "Radio" Waves

Time **Thirty minutes**

MATERIALS

For each small group:

1 air-core transformer

1 Leyden jar

2 electrophori

4 hookup wires

2 pennies (or 2 rounded metal objects or coins)

1 25-watt neon bulb

1 meter stick

1 pair of scissors

1 m of magnet wire (or 1 wire of any kind, insulated or not)

1' of masking tape (or 1' of any kind of tape)

OVERVIEW

Students will use a miniature neon bulb and a homemade antenna to detect electromagnetic radiation that is emitted by an electric arc.

TEACHER BACKGROUND

This lesson is an adaptation of Henrik Hertz's original experiment, which first proved the existence of electromagnetic, or "radio" waves.

The arc produced by the Leyden jar and air-core transformer radiates electromagnetic power in the form of waves. A small neon bulb connected to a short homemade antenna can pick up this radiation and make a greenish spark.

An AM radio can be placed a number of feet away and it, too, will detect the radio waves from the spark, interpreting them as hisses, crackles, and pops.

LAUNCHING THE LESSON

Explain to students that a nineteenth-century mathematician predicted the existence of waves of an electric and magnetic nature. These electromagnetic waves were able to travel through space at the speed of light. As a last lesson, we will peek into this realm of science by recreating the first experiment to prove that electromagnetic waves really exist.

STUDENT ACTIVITY

Have students complete the steps given below:

1. Cut 2 half-meter lengths of wire. Strip 1 or 2 centimeters of insulation from one end of each piece. Twist the stripped sections onto the legs of the neon bulb.

2. Tape the neon bulb and wires to a meter stick, with the neon bulb in the middle and the wires leading to the ends of the meter stick.

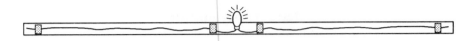

3. Set up the air-core transformer, penny gap, capacitor, and electrophorus, as described in the previous lesson. The gap between pennies should be .5 centimeters.

4. Use the electrophorus to charge the capacitor 100-150 times.

CAUTION
Be careful not to touch the capacitor when it is fully charged.

---

5. Hold the neon bulb on the meter stick about 5 centimeters from the pennies. With the other hand, discharge the capacitor through the air-core transformer. You should see a spark within the neon bulb at the same instant that a spark jumps across the penny gap and a spark is seen on top of the capacitor. (It may help to darken the room.)

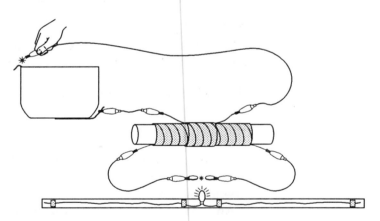

MAKING CONNECTIONS

Students can see that a spark appeared in the neon bulb even though the bulb is in no way attached to the spark gap of the air-core transformer. Somehow, it seems, some electrical energy was transmitted to the neon bulb. Tell the students that this energy is carried as electromagnetic waves, of which radio waves are one kind and visible light another. Explain that this activity was an adaptation of Hertz's experiment of more than a century ago. Challenge students to think of some possible practical uses that might come from this new discovery.

FOR FURTHER INVESTIGATION

Write directives for these activities on chart paper so that groups of students can work on them together:

• Set up a radio nearby and tune it between stations on the AM band. Repeat steps 1-3 from the *Student Activity* section while the radio is on. What do you hear? (Students should hear hisses, crackles, and pops at each step.)

• Experiment with the length and shape of the neon bulb's antenna. What can you do to detect electromagnetic waves as far from the penny gap as possible?

• Make an AM crystal radio from a kit, which is available in most toy stores or hobby shops.

Student Assessment

for Static Electricity

PART A: WRITTEN RESPONSE

Directions: Choose two of the questions below and answer them in as much detail as possible. Use a combination of words and pictures in your explanation.

1. Suppose your teacher were to give you a mystery item. Explain how you would determine if it could produce an electric charge when rubbed.

2. How could you tell if a plastic ruler produces a positive or negative charge?

3. What must happen to a piece of tinsel before it can fly?

4. Explain why the acrylic plate of an electrophorus doesn't need to be re-rubbed every time the pie tin is charged upon it.

5. The electrophorus pie tin, when charged, acquires the opposite charge of the acrylic. Explain how this occurs.

PART B: PROBLEM SOLVING

Directions: Choose two of the problems to solve. Make a list of materials you will need and ask your teacher for help collecting them. When you have a solution, demonstrate it to your teacher.

1. Demonstrate that like charges repel and that a neutral object is attracted to a charged object.

2. Demonstrate that the charges within a neutral object can be imbalanced.

3. Choose five objects: three plastic, one wooden, and one metal. Determine if each is capable of producing an electric charge when rubbed.

4. Using only a charged acrylic rod or plate, give a piece of tinsel a positive charge. Remember that acrylic is negatively charged.

5. Prove that the pie tin and acrylic plate of the electrophorus assume opposite charges.

6. Determine if air is a conductor or an insulator.

7. Devise a method to make a charged electrophorus pie tin discharge slowly, over at least two seconds, rather than in an instant spark.

Student Assessment

for Current Electricity

PART A: WRITTEN RESPONSE

Directions: Choose two of the questions below and answer them in as much detail as possible. Use a combination of words and pictures in your explanation.

1. Twenty fresh D-cells, each 1.5 volts, are connected in parallel. Although you might expect this large parallel battery to shock when you touch its terminals, it won't. Explain why. Then tell what you can do to make the battery shock.

2. Suppose you are given four resistors, each shaped like a cylinder and made of the same material. The first resistor is short and fat, the second long and fat, the third short and thin, and the fourth long and thin. Which will resist the electron flow the most? Why? Which will allow electrons to pass through it most easily? Why?

3. Explain how a cell of copper, zinc, and vinegar produces an electron flow.

4. What is the relationship between the voltage, amperage, and resistance of a circuit?

5. Why will three cells connected in series melt a strand of steel wool faster than one cell alone?

PART B: PROBLEM SOLVING

Directions: Choose two of the problems to solve. Make a list of materials you will need and ask your teacher for help collecting them. When you have a solution, demonstrate it to your teacher.

1. Demonstrate two ways in which the current produced by a voltaic pile is like the current produced by a capacitor.

2. Make chlorine gas from salt water.

3. Build a 10-cell voltaic pile. Prove that it produces an electron flow.

4. Use electricity to heat a piece of aluminum foil.

5. Does wet, salty skin resist more or less than dry skin? Provide evidence to support your answer.

Student Assessment

for Electromagnetism

PART A: WRITTEN RESPONSE

Directions: Choose two of the questions below and answer them in as much detail as possible. Use a combination of words and pictures in your explanation.

1. A boy tries to make an electromagnet that can pick up his toy car. Unfortunately, the electromagnet is too weak. What advice can you give him to make his electromagnet stronger?
2. Explain how the electromagnet turns itself off and on in a buzzer circuit.
3. How does a buzz-tone telephone transmit tones through a wire?
4. How can you use a magnet to create an electron flow?
5. What are three practical uses for the electromagnet? Carefully describe what the electromagnet does in each example you mention.

PART B: PROBLEM SOLVING

Directions: Choose two of the problems to solve. Make a list of materials you will need and ask your teacher for help collecting them. When you have a solution, demonstrate it to your teacher.

1. Prove that an electron flow can create a magnetic force.
2. Does the orientation of an electromagnet's north and south poles depend upon which direction the electrons flow through the wire? Design an experiment to find out.
3. Build a device that uses electromagnetism to communicate.
4. Prove that a magnet can create an electron flow.
5. Transmit and detect electromagnetic radiation.

Finding Materials

acrylic plates You can obtain acrylic plates from Cuisenaire. Call 1-800-237-3142 and ask for item number 080008. You may also find them in a plastics store (check your yellow pages). Explain that you are a teacher and ask to look through the recycle bin. A fair price for scrap acrylic is about 20 cents per pound. If you have to buy new pieces, save money by getting the thinnest sheets available.

acrylic rods You will almost certainly have to buy these, but they are worth buying. (You might first try looking in the plastics store recycle bin.) Buy rods at least ¼-inch in diameter and 1 foot long. You can save money by purchasing acrylic tubes of the same diameter, but expect the tubes to wear out slightly faster than the rods.

copper sheets You can obtain copper sheets from Cuisenaire. Call 1-800-237-3142 and ask for item number 080009. (The standard size is 12 x 12 inches, and between .5 and 1.0 mm thick.) You may also be able to buy copper sheet from a roofer or a good building supply store.

emery cloth You can obtain emery cloth from Cuisenaire. Call 1-800-237-3142 and ask for item number 080010. It is also available at almost any hardware store. This item is often mistaken for sandpaper; however, emery cloth has a cloth back and lasts longer than sandpaper. Try to buy emery cloth with a fine grain.

high-density polyethylene The heart of the Leyden jar is almost certainly in your home right now. Most plastic gallon milk jugs, baby-wipe containers, shampoo bottles, and motor-oil bottles are high-density polyethylene, and will make good Leyden jars. (In fact, anything with a recycle code "2" printed on it is made of high-density polyethylene.) If you want to be sure you have high-density polyethylene, however, buy a roll of it at a hardware or paint store. For about 5 dollars, you should get enough to make a class set of Leyden jars.

hookup wires Each of these consists of an insulated wire, approximately 18 gauge, 12 to 18 inches long, with an alligator clip on each end. (These are also commonly called test leads, test wires, alligator-clip wires, jumper cables, or connecting wires.) You can either buy premade test leads, or make your own. For premade leads, call Cuisenaire at 1-800-237-3142 and ask for item number 082018. To make your own, buy the wire and alligator clips separately at an auto-parts store and solder them together. In most cases, you can improvise around the need for test leads by using strips of aluminum foil and masking tape.

magnet wire You can obtain magnet wire from Cuisenaire. Call 1-800-237-3142 and ask for item number 080011. You may be able to buy a larger spool for less by finding a local distributor. If you can't find a distributor in the yellow pages, try calling the Phelps-Dodge Magnet Wire Company (212-458-4444) for one of their local distributors. (Almost any electronics store will carry magnet wire, but you will pay a premium for convenience.)

steel nut, bolt, and washers Available at any hardware store, the best for our purpose is the nonhardened variety—happily, the cheapest and most common. Look on the bolt's head. If there are no radial lines, it is the nonhardened kind.

tinsel This item is available through Cuisenaire. Call 1-800-237-3142 and ask for item number 082042. Tinsel is also available in any grocery or drugstore around Christmas and in craft stores throughout the year. Look for the thinnest (and usually the cheapest) metallic tinsel available.

transformer This item is available at any electronics store. If you prefer, you can save 5 dollars by salvaging one from a broken radio. (Any radio that plugs into a wall outlet will have a transformer.)

wool cloths The best are made from old, heavy 100 percent wool shirts. Find the shirts at thrift shops and cut each into about 15 cloths.

zinc sheet Zinc sheets are available through Cuisenaire by calling 1-800-237-3142 and requesting item number 080012. The standard size is 12 x 12 inches, and between .5 and 1 millimeter thick.

Glossary

ampere The unit of *quantity* of electron flow. One ampere is defined as the number of electrons, or amount of current, that flows through one ohm of resistance when one volt is applied.

atom The tiniest building block of nature from which everything is made. Atoms are incredibly small. (This paper is approximately 5 million atoms thick.) An atom itself is made up of three main parts: proton, neutron, and electron (which are themselves made of even more basic parts).

battery Two or more cells, connected in series or parallel, working together.

capacitor The modern name for the Leyden jar, a simple device that stores an electric charge. Most capacitors are made out of two layers of foil separated by an insulator.

cell Two metal plates, such as zinc and copper, separated by a conducting liquid such as vinegar, salt water, or sulfuric acid.

charged An overall excess of electrons or an overall lack of electrons. For example, when a balloon becomes charged, there are extra electrons on its surface.

circuit The path that electrons take as they flow from the negative to positive terminal of a battery, or cell. See *open circuit* and *closed circuit*.

closed circuit A circuit in which there are no breaks and through which electrons flow.

conductor A substance that will allow electrons to pass through it.

current Often used interchangeably with *electron flow*, it actually means the size of the flow of an electric charge from positive to negative.

electrode The part of the electrolysis circuit that emits or collects the electrons.

electrolysis The chemical change produced by an electron flow. For example, salt water can be changed into chlorine gas and hydrogen gas by an electron flow.

electrolyte The solution in which electrolysis takes place. It contains positive and negative ions (charged atoms or molecules) and conducts electricity as these ions flow.

electromagnet A device that creates a magnetic force when electrons flow through it.

electromagnetic induction The production of an electron flow by a moving magnetic force.

electromagnetic waves Waves created by the rapid movement of an electric or magnetic force that pass through space or matter. Radio waves, visible light, and x-rays are all kinds of electromagnetic waves.

electron The negatively-charged part of the atom. The electron loosely orbits the nucleus of the atom. It is relatively easy to remove an electron from many kinds of atoms.

electron flow The movement of electrons through a circuit.

electron flow The movement of electrons through a circuit.

electrophorus A simple device consisting of a pie plate with an insulated handle, a piece of acrylic, and a wool rag; used to produce and transport a charge.

electroscope A simple instrument that allows you to "see" a charge. In *Flying Tinsel*, one piece of tinsel is suspended through a paper clip and the tinsel is charged. After observing that the two leaves repel each other, students conclude that they both carry the same charge and that like charges repel.

ground A large conductor that a charge can "spread out" in. The earth is the biggest and most commonly used ground: hence, its name.

induction The creation of an imbalance of charges within a conductor caused by a nearby charge.

insulator A substance that does not let electrons flow through it.

Leyden jar The first capacitor, consisting of a jar coated with foil on the inside and outside. The Leyden jar, now known as the capacitor, is capable of storing an electric charge.

like charges Two or more charges that are the same—either both positive or both negative. Like charges repel each other.

negative The charge of an electron.

open circuit A circuit with a "break" that prevents electrons from flowing.

parallel The connection of two or more devices such as resistors or cells so that electrons can flow through either independently of the other. Contrasts with *series*.

positive The charge of a proton.

proton The source of the positive charge in an atom, located in the nucleus.

resist To hold back, or oppose, an electron flow.

resistance Expressed in ohms(Í), the extent to which a substance opposes, or holds back, an electron flow.

resistor A substance that holds back, or resists an electron flow.

series The connection of devices such as resistors or cells that cause electrons to flow through each device in turn. Contrasts with parallel.

static electricity An electric charge that does not move. It is best understood in contrast to current electricity, in which charges are constantly in motion.

terminal The top or bottom plate in a voltaic pile, or the positive or negative end of a battery.

transformer A device that uses electromagnetic induction to produce a secondary current of relatively high or low voltage from an alternating primary current.

unlike charges Two opposite charges—one positive and one negative. Unlike charges attract.

vibration A rapid back-and-forth movement. Vibrations that repeat with a frequency between 20 and 20,000 beats per second can be heard as tones.

volt The unit of electrical pressure, or pushing force. One copper-zinc-vinegar cell delivers approximately one volt. (Note that the volt is not a measure of the number of electrons.)

voltage Electrical pressure, or pushing force on a charge.